BEYOND THE RODNEY KING STORY

Prepared by

Charles J. Ogletree, Jr.
Mary Prosser
Abbe Smith
William Talley, Jr.

Criminal Justice Institute at Harvard Law School
for the National Association
for the Advancement of Colored People

NORTHEASTERN UNIVERSITY PRESS

BOSTON

BEYOND

THE

RODNEY

KING

STORY

An Investigation

of Police Conduct

in Minority

Communities

Advisor in Criminal Justice to Northeastern University Press
Gil Geis

Northeastern University Press

Library of Congress Cataloging-in-Publication Data

Beyond the Rodney King story : an investigation of police conduct in
minority communities / [prepared by Charles J. Ogletree . . . et al.;
Criminal Justice Institute at Harvard Law School for the National
Association for the Advancement of Colored People].
p. cm.
"At the conclusion of the public hearings, the NAACP selected the
Criminal Justice Institute of Harvard Law School, and the Trotter
Institute of the University of Massachusetts, to review the material
that had been collected and write a report."
Includes bibliographical references.
ISBN 1-55553-202-0 (hard : alk. paper)
1. Police—United States—Complaints against. 2. Discrimination
in law enforcement—United States. 3. Public relations—United
States—Police. 4. Afro-Americans—Civil rights—United States.
I. Ogletree, Charles J. II. Harvard Law School. Criminal Justice
Institute. III. National Association for the Advancement of Colored
People. IV. William Monroe Trotter Institute.
HV8141.B49 1994
363.2'32'0973—dc20 94-30409

Designed by Liz Doles

Composed in Utopia by Coghill Composition Company in
Richmond, Virginia. Printed and bound by The Maple Press in
York, Pennsylvania. The paper is Sebago, an acid-free sheet.

MANUFACTURED IN THE UNITED STATES OF AMERICA

98 97 96 95 94   5 4 3 2 1

▲ ACKNOWLEDGMENTS ▲

The Harvard Law School Criminal Justice Institute and the NAACP gratefully acknowledge and thank the William Monroe Trotter Institute of the University of Massachusetts at Boston and its staff, including James Jennings, Harold W. Horton, Suzanne M. Baker, Cheryl H. Brown, George Cox, Aileen Felder, Fred D. Johnson, and Crystal McFall for their valuable contributions to portions of this report.

The Harvard Law School Criminal Justice Institute is grateful to Ann Ashton, Jenifer Bensinger, Carmia Caesar, Christa Evereteze, Sally Greenberg, Anthony Grumbach, Letitia Johnson, William Lee, Christopher Lenzo, Susan Michaelson, Andrea Phillips, Martin Rosenthal, Seth Rosenthal, Melissa Scott, and Melody Webb for their contributions to this book, as well as family, friends, and students for putting up with us throughout the project. We especially thank Mo Griffin and Jamie Wright at the Criminal Justice Institute for their many significant contributions to this project.

The NAACP acknowledges with gratitude the outstanding cooperation received from elected officials, law enforcement personnel, and private citizens in the course of the police conduct hearings. We are especially grateful to the local officers and members of the NAACP branches in the cities we visited for their invaluable assistance, including Paul Riddick, Norman Seay, Johnnie McMillian, A. D. Pinckney, Joseph Duff, Keryl Smith, and Judge Alexander Green. The NAACP also wishes to thank its staff, including Jack Gravely, Hearings Coordinator; Dennis Courtland Hayes, General Counsel; William H. Penn, Director, Branch and Field Services; and Janice Washington, Assistant Director, Branch and Field Services.

▲ CONTENTS ▲

African Americans' attitudes toward the police have long been marked by ambivalence—and for understandable reasons. On the one hand, they have wanted the defenders of law and justice to provide them the same protection from crime and criminals as that afforded other citizens. On the other hand, there has been a corroding fear that because of their race the possibility is always present that any encounter with the police, no matter how innocent, carries the risk of abuse, mistreatment, or even death. Rare indeed is the black male, and in some instances the black female, who has grown to adulthood in America without having suffered some unpleasant experience at the hands of the police, especially white police.

No one can deny that law-enforcement officers have a tough job. In the face of the constant threat of danger, they must wear many different hats while maintaining the peace. They nobly serve as our fragile bridge between competing interests and the rule of law. Where would we be without the police? One thing is certain. Where there is a sour relationship between the police and the African American community, the best interests of both are jeopardized—the police, from the perspective of their sworn duty to uphold the law and keep the peace; the community, from the standpoint of its desire for safety and freedom from fear.

The two need to work together. When they are separated by a wall of mistrust and suspicion, each is at a disadvantage and the legitimate concerns of both are undermined.

Despite the good job that most police officers do, one of the constants in the almost nine-decade history of the National Association for the Advancement of Colored People has been complaints about police misconduct toward African Americans. The ink was hardly dry on its 1909 charter when the NAACP, in 1910, undertook its very first legal action—the defense of a poor, black Arkansas sharecropper, Pink Franklin, who had sought to protect his home against an illegal, predawn police raid.

We cannot ignore the sobering reality that the relationship between the police and black communities is a continuing source of friction. In almost every major urban rebellion of the last three decades, it was some police action directed against African Americans that was the precipitating cause of civil disorder: New York City in 1964; Los Angeles in 1965; Cleveland, 1966; Newark and Detroit, 1967; Los Angeles, 1992.

When the National Advisory Commission on Civil Disorders, commonly called the Kerner Commission, made its report on the events of the long, hot summer of 1967, it found "police actions were 'final' incidents before the outbreak of violence in 12 of the 24 surveyed disorders."[1]

It would be unfair to hold the police totally at fault. They may have unconsciously supplied the match, but they did not lay the kindling. Obviously, there were other, deep-seated factors at work, such as hopelessness, frustration, and anger at the system, spawned by the progenitors race and poverty.

Yet, police-community relations are not to be disregarded as a factor contributing to community unrest. As the Kerner Commission concluded: "The abrasive relationship between the police and the minority communities has been a major— and explosive—source of grievance, tension and disorder."

Calling on some of the best minds in the country, the commission outlined a blueprint for addressing the problems it had identified. Included were the following recommendations:

▲ Review police operations "in the ghetto, to ensure proper conduct by individual officers and eliminate abrasive practices."[2]

▲ Provide "more adequate police protection of ghetto residents, to eliminate the . . . high sense of insecurity"[3] and the belief in the existence of a dual standard of law enforcement.[4]

▲ Establish fair and effective mechanisms for the redress of grievances against the police, and other municipal employees.[5]

▲ Develop and adopt policy guidelines to assist officers in making critical decisions "in areas where police conduct can create tension."[6]

▲ Develop and use innovative programs to ensure widespread "community support for law enforcement."[7]

That was a quarter century ago. As with so many of the other sensible recommendations made in the Kerner Report, however, those dealing with the police and minority communities have not been acted upon in any meaningful way. Apparently, the psychologist Kenneth Clark was prophetic when he testified to the commission that urban riots, repeated every few years throughout this century in America, have "prompted the same analysis, the same recommendations, and the same inaction." America is detrimentally falling prey to this pattern— that is, after the urgency of a disastrous event has faded, the circumstances that helped produce the event are forgotten until a new disaster occurs to reveal that what was broken before has not been fixed. Thus, it was a case of shock déjà vu when so much of America saw the amateur videotape recording of the beating of motorist Rodney King in March 1991. Things like this were not supposed to happen.

With the Rodney King episode as the catalyst, the NAACP announced at its 1991 annual convention in Houston that it would conduct a series of national hearings into police conduct. The purpose of the inquiry was to provide a public platform for citizens, government officials, community leaders, law-enforcement personnel, and related experts to detail whether and why they believe there continues to exist a wall of mistrust between African American communities and law-enforcement departments and to indicate what positive steps should be taken to correct this morbid condition.

Six cities, from the NAACP's seven-region structure, were selected as host sites—Norfolk, Miami, Los Angeles, Houston, St. Louis, and Indianapolis. The hearings were not cursory, beginning early in the morning and usually ending late at night.

A special word of thanks is due the national staff members who constituted the Hearing Panel and spent countless hours in preparation for the implementation of the hearings—Dennis Courtland Hayes, general counsel; William H. Penn, director of branch and field services; Janice Washington, assistant director of branch and field services; and Jack Gravely, director of special projects, who was also coordinator of the hearings. Technical assistance was provided to the panel by James D. Williams, the NAACP's director of public relations.

In each of the cities, the panel was joined by at least one representative from the host local NAACP branch. Because of his or her intimate knowledge of the city, each of these persons made invaluable contributions. Our appreciation to the Honorable Alexander Green, president, Houston Branch; Keryl Burgess Smith, executive director, Houston Branch; Paul Riddick, president, Norfolk Branch; Johnnie McMillian, president, Miami Branch; Norman R. Seay, legal redress chairman, St. Louis Branch; Joseph Duff, Esq., president, Los Angeles Branch; and Dr. A. D. Pinckney, president, Indianapolis Branch.

The NAACP made clear at the beginning of each hearing that it was not engaged in any form of police bashing but had, rather, come in search of information. Once the voluminous testimony and documents had been gathered, the difficult process of analyzing data began. To assist the NAACP in the development of a final report, we selected two outstanding institutions—the Criminal Justice Institute of the Harvard Law School, and the William Monroe Trotter Institute of the University of Massachusetts at Boston—to examine the transcripts and documents with an eye toward offering some preliminary recommendations. We are grateful for their invaluable input and assistance.

While our hearings were being held and our report compiled, fourteen months passed between the time of Mr. King's beating and a Simi Valley, California, jury's finding that none of the officers bore any guilt. The faith of many in the minority community in Los Angeles was shattered when the verdicts of acquittal came in—the system had let them down again. Many of them could see themselves or their loved ones in Rodney King's shoes, and they were chilled by the thought that what had happened to him could happen to them.

The NAACP National Office press release on the verdict read:

African-Americans and many others are grieved by this inexplicable miscarriage of justice that will reinforce the belief that there is a double standard of justice when race enters the picture. We are bitter and disappointed at the outcome but we urge that the decision be met with calmness.

When disorder broke out in Los Angeles, we condemned the acts of violence and destruction. Nonetheless, our initial grief and disappointment were bolstered by the findings of the Independent Commission on the Los Angeles Police Department. Formed after the beating of Mr. King, and chaired by Warren Christopher, now United States secretary of state, the commission's report of July 1991 stated:

> Testimony from a wide variety of witnesses depicts the LAPD as an organization with practices and procedures that are conducive to discriminatory treatment and officer misconduct directed to members of minority groups.[8]
> Witnesses repeatedly told of LAPD officers verbally harassing minorities, detaining African-American and Latino men who fit certain generalized descriptions of suspects, employing unnecessarily invasive or humiliating tactics in minority neighborhoods and using excessive force.[9]
> While the Commission does not purport to adjudicate the validity of any one of these numerous complaints, the intensity and frequency of them reveal a serious problem.[10]

Our own hearings had been completed by the time the city erupted in the spring of 1992. Steeped in documents produced by the hearings, we were already aware from testimonies given that the "problem" was not confined to Los Angeles. In every city we visited, we found the climate there replicated in varying degrees. The testimony of one witness, Rev. Anthony Lee of Indianapolis—the heart of mid-America—is chilling:

Rodney King and his family . . . are blessed, because had they
been in Indianapolis he would have been killed. They kill
you here. They don't just beat you. He would have been killed.
And his family would have been slapped in the face by giving the officer who shot him an award of valor. . . . It's appalling.
The travesty. This kind of thing is going on in 1990. . . . It's
just abusive. It's just disrespect for black life across the board
on every level in this town. . . . It's just horrible. I cannot
overstate it.[11]

As we heard the voices of citizens, we also heard the voices
of those responsible for law enforcement. Overall, we were im-
pressed by their willingness to admit that police-community
relations are not what they should be. There was a sensitivity
in those who appeared that we found encouraging.

One example came from Janet Reno, then state's attorney
for Dade County, Florida, and now U.S. attorney general. In
response to a question as to whether she felt there was a perception in minority communities that they receive unfair or
harsher treatment from police, Ms. Reno responded in the affirmative. Expanding on why that perception exists, she went
on to say:

I think you start first from the whole base of the charge of racism over the history of this nation, of this community, . . .
socio-economic conditions . . . exist and there is injustice . . .
even independent of racism. . . .[12]

[A]nybody acting in authority has to be very careful and
there have to be checks and balances developed to ensure
that they're responsive.[13]

I think one of the areas that I see [as] less [problematic is
when] your police officers are known in the community and

work in the community. I think that has to be one of the keys
to what we do. We have been advocating for some time a
team approach; not just a team policing but identifying neighborhoods and carving out a small enough neighborhood
where we can really return to one on one contact; have a top
flight public health nurse, . . . social worker, and community
respected police officer assigned as a team making a commitment to that narrowed community for five years and then
expanding on that community.[14]

And I think that is what is necessary to overcome a history
of economic, social and racial injustice.[15]

Almost without exception, one criterion advocated by virtually every law-enforcement officer appearing before our panel
was "better relationships with the people we serve."

We doubt that such statements would have been so freely
made not too long ago, which gives rise to some hope on our
part that perhaps there is a new breed of law-enforcement personnel ascending to positions of leadership—those who are
much more sensitive to the dynamics of minority communities
and much less wedded to a philosophy of "us versus them."

The difficulty, as we see it, will be how this attitude gets con-
veyed, transferred, or trickled down into the rank and file,
where most incidents of misconduct have their origin. This was
one of the core issues that emerged from our hearings, and it
is a problem that has to be solved if we are ever to bridge the
chasm that now separates the police and the black community.

As the African American community again raises its voice in
a demand for equal justice, we looked beyond the Rodney King
story to the larger issue of police-community relations
throughout the United States. Our findings and recommenda-

tions in this report herald a new concept for policing in the twenty-first century. We have made an honest effort to address a condition that imperils us all. The question we now pose is: Is anyone listening, does anyone care?

Benjamin L. Hooks
Executive Director/CEO
National Association for the Advancement of Colored People
1977–93

NOTES

1 REPORT OF THE NATIONAL ADVISORY COMMISSION ON CIVIL DISORDERS 70 (1968).
2 *Id.* at 158.
3 *Id.*
4 *Id.* at 161.
5 *Id.* at 158.
6 *Id.*
7 *Id.* at 158, 165–68.
8 REPORT OF THE INDEPENDENT COMMISSION ON THE LOS ANGELES POLICE DEPARTMENT, at xii (1991).
9 *Id.*
10 *Id.* at xii–xiii.
11 Testimony of Rev. Anthony Lee, Genesis Christian Mission, INDIANAPOLIS HEARINGS, December 18, 1991, at 317–20.
12 Testimony of Janet Reno, Dade County state's attorney, MIAMI HEARINGS, November 12, 1991, at 17.
13 *Id.*
14 *Id.* at 17–18.
15 *Id.* at 18.

BEYOND THE RODNEY KING STORY

INTRODUCTION

A NAACP, CJI, Trotter

The National Association for the Advancement of Colored People (NAACP) is the nation's oldest and largest civil rights organization. Founded in 1909 to empower and protect African Americans under the Constitution through the exercise of principles of equal justice under the law, the NAACP has more than half a million members, enrolled in some twenty-one hundred branches in the fifty states, the District of Columbia, and abroad. The association has been instrumental since its early days in securing passage of all civil rights legislation in this century, and it remains committed to the full enforcement of these laws. The NAACP also utilizes the executive, legislative, and judicial processes to ensure equity and fairness in such areas as housing, employment, voting, political representation, education, health care, and the administration of justice.

The Criminal Justice Institute (CJI) is Harvard Law School's first curriculum-based clinical program in the criminal justice area. Created in 1990, CJI offers practice, education, and research opportunities in criminal justice to Harvard law students, as well as providing a wide range of services to national and local communities. The staff of CJI has published articles on a wide range of issues concerning criminal law, the criminal justice system, and clinical education, and members teach law students to provide high-quality representation to indigent persons in criminal cases. Members of the CJI staff have also served as consultants on criminal justice projects covering a range of topics, including public defenders, the right to counsel, habeas corpus, the death penalty, police conduct, commutation for battered women convicted of killing abusive partners, youth violence, and alternatives to incarceration.

The William Monroe Trotter Institute, established in 1984 at the University of Massachusetts at Boston, supports research, publications, and forums of major concern to the African American community. The institute grew out of several interests: the desire of the University of Massachusetts at Boston to enhance African American studies at the university; the university's mission of service to its urban constituency; and the need for policy research focusing on the African American experience in metropolitan Boston and New England.

The Trotter Institute conducts research to influence public policy on issues of concern to African Americans and undertakes academic projects to improve understanding of the history, culture, and social development of the black community. The institute also offers technical assistance to community and neighborhood organizations through the sponsorship of public policy forums and conferences and consulting services.

B Methodology of the Report

The March 3, 1991, beating of African American motorist Rodney King, fortuitously captured on videotape, and the subsequent state and federal prosecutions of the four white police officers involved brought national attention to the long-neglected problem of the excessive use of police force in minority communities. The NAACP has a long-standing interest in the problem of police misconduct, and the Rodney King incident sparked a renewed response.

On July 9, 1991, at the request of Executive Director Benjamin Hooks, the NAACP announced that it would sponsor a series of national hearings on police conduct and community relations. These were held in Norfolk, Virginia, on November 6, 1991; Miami, Florida, on November 12–13, 1991; Houston, Texas, on November 19–20, 1991; Los Angeles, California, on December 3–4, 1991; St. Louis, Missouri, on December 6, 1991; and Indianapolis, Indiana, on December 17–18, 1991.

In each city, the NAACP Commission, which functioned as a hearing board, was composed of association members Dennis Hayes, general counsel; Jack Gravely, director of special projects and hearings coordinator; William Penn, Sr., director of branch and field services; Janice Washington, assistant director of branch and field services; and a local representative of the NAACP. Various public officials, police department representatives, criminal justice experts, members of community organizations, and citizens appeared before the NAACP Commission and offered testimony concerning police conduct in their communities.

At the conclusion of the public hearings, the NAACP selected the Criminal Justice Institute of Harvard Law School, and the William Monroe Trotter Institute of the University of Massachusetts at Boston, to review the material that had been collected and to write a report. The report would be issued in March 1993. The methodology used in its preparation consisted of examining the transcripts of the public hearings, categorizing and reporting the information, analyzing the findings, consulting the scholarly work that has been done in the field, and offering some preliminary recommendations.

C Police Conduct and Community Relations: Defining the Problem

While the impetus for this report was the beating of Rodney King in Los Angeles, his case is not unique. The unusual aspect of what happened to Rodney King was that it was *videotaped;* unfortunately, episodes of police beatings of black citizens happen in cities and towns all over this country without being recorded. The November 5, 1992, fatal beating of Malice Green by four police officers in Detroit[1]—to name one such case— suggests that little has been learned from the Rodney King incident.

On March 20 and April 17, 1991, the United States House of Representatives Committee on the Judiciary, Subcommittee on Civil and Constitutional Rights, held hearings on the issue of police brutality. In its report on H.R. 3371 (a bill relating to civil injunctive relief for unlawful conduct by law-enforcement officers), the committee acknowledged widespread police misconduct in Los Angeles. The report stated that there are a significant number of officers in the Los Angeles Police Department (LAPD) who regularly use excessive force and that their conduct was well known to police department management, which condoned the behavior through lax supervision and inadequate investigation of complaints. These findings were based upon studies conducted in connection with the Christopher Commission Report.[2]

The House committee reported that the situation is not limited to Los Angeles. According to police chiefs from ten major cities, law-enforcement organizations, and other experts, excessive force in American policing is a frequent occurrence, particularly in our inner cities, and complaints that minority residents are the objects of disrespect and abuse are widespread.

The Judiciary Committee concluded, as does the NAACP in this report, that policing is difficult, dangerous work and that most officers do not abuse their authority. On the contrary, the majority of police officers are dedicated women and men who strive to uphold the ideals of the Constitution. Under growing hardship and danger, most police officers make an enormous contribution to public safety and deserve the nation's gratitude. Incidents of restraint in the face of provocation greatly outnumber incidents of brutality. However, given the extensive evidence of widespread and often racially motivated use of excessive force, police departments, local authorities, and state and federal governments have a responsibility to respond.

Whether or not police misconduct is increasing—something that is impossible to document, given a historical failure to report most misconduct for a host of reasons—it cannot be denied that a wall of mistrust exists between minority groups and the police, and that the relationship between the police and the community has eroded considerably. Recent poll results are quite telling. According to a 1991 survey, 59 percent of those responding believe that police brutality is common in some or most communities in the United States, and 53 percent think that police are more likely to use excessive force against black or Hispanic suspects than against white suspects.[3]

The results are even more disturbing when they are broken

down into responses by race. When asked whether they agreed or disagreed with the statement, "These days police in most cities treat blacks as fairly as they treat whites," 45 percent of white adults agreed and 45 percent disagreed, whereas 73 percent of black adults disagreed.[4] Among black adults, 66 percent believe that black persons charged with crimes are treated more harshly in our justice system than white persons charged with crimes.[5] Only 34 percent of white adults hold the same view.[6] In New York City, 33 percent of white adults believe that police favor whites over blacks; 65 percent of the black adults believe the police favor whites over blacks.[7]

According to the *Statistical Record of Black America*,[8] 60 percent of white adults think, in general, that the police do a "good" job against crime. Only 39 percent of blacks and 44 percent of Hispanics agree. In a poll of high school seniors, only 22.6 percent of blacks (as compared to 40.5 percent of white students) believe that police are doing a "good" or "very good" job for the country as a whole. More than one-third (37.7 percent) of the black students polled further stated that there are "considerable" or "great" problems of dishonesty and immorality in the leadership of the police and other law-enforcement agencies, and only 33 percent rated the honesty and ethical standards of police officers as "high" or "very high."

Respect for law is the cornerstone of a free society. The rule of law is built upon the consent of people who believe the laws are administered fairly, thus commanding respect and confidence. Unjust or discriminatory administration of law involving excessive force tends only to create distrust and contempt for the law and for those who enforce it.

The role of the police is difficult, dangerous, demanding, and often misunderstood. Urban problems have intensified police problems, requiring increased resources and community support. Maintaining a police force at sufficient size, with adequate training, equipment, and morale, is increasingly difficult. In lower-income areas, where the problems of unemployment, poor education, inadequate housing, and drugs are rampant, the position of the police officer is especially difficult because he or she is often viewed as a symbol of oppression. The police officer is seen as a buffer between disadvantaged groups and advantaged groups.

The NAACP recognizes the noble and thankless job performed by police officers, often at great personal risk. The NAACP recognizes that inadequate resources, equipment, training, and support undermine the best-intentioned officers. It is important that the public realize that conflict is part of police work. Law enforcement means the loss of liberty for some; often, this is not a happy event. As police do their job, there will be complaints about what they do and how they do it. However, when they act fairly, lawfully, and without bias they must be supported.

It is in this spirit that the NAACP held public hearings in six cities, collected data, consulted with experts, and offers the following findings and recommendations.

D The Importance of Race

The inseparability of racism and policing in the United States

[R]acism is not an automatic thing. It's an organized prejudice against people. Racism, you just don't come out and be this way.

It's got to be some motivation behind it. . . . I'm saying racism is unnatural. . . . It's a system. . . .[9]

I'm speaking here today [because of] police brutality to myself. This police officer came right up and pull[ed] up behind me. . . . He pull[ed] me out of the car . . . grabbed my head and slammed it into the [car] . . . blood [ran] down my lip . . . he broke my chain. . . . And he kept saying "Yeah nigger, run now nigger." . . . [H]e started to hit me in my stomach, hit me in the side. . . . The guy kept on punching and hitting. . . . [He] pull[ed] [his] revolver . . . slammed me upside the head with it. . . . [He] kept hitting and kept kicking. . . . [H]e turned and pointed the gun right at me [and said], "[R]un now nigger. . . ."[10]

Race, police, and violence are as one in this country. Images of crime are inextricably connected to images of African Americans. The desire for police protection is tied to the fear of who might wander into the neighborhood without it. The police, with their finest artillery of radio patrol cars, helicopters, advanced surveillance equipment, and high-tech weaponry, are no more than one little boy, finger in the dike, trying to hold back the flood of frustration and anger born of a history of racism and despair.

It is impossible to study the police in this country without studying race. It is impossible to understand the police conduct in the Rodney King beating—or the daily incidents of police "use of force"—without understanding the history of police-minority relations. Those who claim that the verdict in the "first Rodney King case" can be explained as one that was not racist, but "pro-police," should next try to separate land from sea. Can they really say where the one ends and the other begins?

Those who unflinchingly defend the police, no matter the misconduct alleged, often do so out of a need and fear that grows out of a deep racism that has become part of the fabric of American life. The need is for protection, safety, security, the lack of "disturbance." But protection from whom? Safe and secure from whom? Undisturbed by the presence of whom? The fear at one time might have been of criminals like Charles Manson, Gary Gilmore, or Ted Bundy, or of newer versions like John Wayne Gacy or Jeffrey Dahmer. Truth is, the unapologetic embrace of police power in the Rodney King case, and in much of America, has more to do with Willie Horton than even the most sensational white killer. America, and especially white America, believes it needs the police to protect it from violent black men.

Recommendations for change in the way police departments conduct their business necessarily include recommendations for broader social change. While there is a need for "crime control"—the detection of crime, and the apprehension and prosecution of those who commit it[11]—it is clear that law enforcement alone does little or nothing to reduce crime and violence.[12] There is a much more fundamental need for crime *prevention:* addressing the causes of crime and violence.[13] Unfortunately, getting to the root of the causes of criminal violence—which includes addressing poverty, unemployment, inequality, and the loss of community—is not as popular as longer prison sentences, new prison construction, and capital punishment.

The recommendations contained in this report rest on the premise that the police, and notions of acceptable police conduct, are very much the product of a racist society. The beating of Rodney King is part of a long and shameful history of racially motivated brutality and degradation that continue to find expression in powerful places.

Racism, deprivation, and marginalization

I look at the T.V.
Your America's doing well
I look out the window
My America's catching hell
I just want to know which way do I go to get to your America?
I just want to know which way do I go to get to your America?
I change the channel
Your America's doing fine
I read the headlines
My America's doing time[14]

I think white America has to be jolted into reality: if we do not devote the resources necessary to avert the tragedy, we'll become a police state. Crime will acquire more and more racial overtones. Will there have to be some sort of explosion, some sort of civil disorder, before we realize the gravity of the situation?[15]

We live in a time of intense racial polarity, which, notwithstanding the progress made by many African Americans, seems to be getting worse, not better. Racial divisiveness does not merely "trickle down" from those in power; it pours. When unemployment is said to be caused by affirmative action, the sagging economy by poor, unwed mothers on welfare, and urban unrest by now discontinued social programs that sought to revitalize inner cities, there is a clear message about who is on one side and who is on the other.

While the police did not invent racial division or racism in

America, they play an integral part in perpetuating the chasm between black and white life.

> When white people hear the cry, "the police are coming!" for them it almost always means, "help is on the way." Black citizens cannot make the same assumption. If you have been the victim of a crime, you cannot presume that the police will actually show up; or, if they do, that they will take much note of your losses or suffering. . . . If you are black and young and a man, the arrival of the police does not usually signify help, but something very different. . . . You may be a college student and sing in a church choir, but that will not overcome the police presumption that you have probably done something they can arrest you for.[16]

The fact is that race is a primary factor in American life and in the criminal justice system. While African Americans make up between 12 and 13 percent of the general population, they are disproportionately represented in every aspect of the criminal system as offenders, victims, prisoners, and arrestees.[17] Black men and women account for 47 percent of the individuals awaiting trial in local jails or serving short sentences there. They make up 45.3 percent of state and federal prison inmates and comprise 40.1 percent of prisoners sentenced to death.[18] Approximately one in four African American males between the ages of twenty and twenty-nine is incarcerated, on probation, or on parole.[19] Overall, more than a million African Americans are either behind bars or a "violation" away from prison.[20]

There is no question that racial bias plays a role in the disproportionate numbers of African Americans arrested.[21] Notwithstanding the realization of the Supreme Court twenty-five years ago in *Terry v. Ohio*[22] that the power of the police to stop and frisk could be used as a tool against minorities, race remains "one of the most salient criteria to patrol [officers] in deciding whether to stop someone."[23] Blacks are likelier than whites to be stopped, interrogated, arrested, prosecuted, convicted, and sentenced to prison.[24]

Blacks are disproportionately represented among police shooting casualties. In one five-month period in Miami and Dade County, there were ten fatal shootings by police. Nine of those shot were people of color.[25] In New York City, where whites are 64.1% of the population and blacks are 20.5%, blacks are victims in 60.4% of police shootings.[26] Nationally, between 1976 and 1987, some 1,800 black persons and about 3,000 whites were killed by law-enforcement officers.[27] The figures reveal that black Americans have a three times greater chance than whites of being killed by a police bullet.[28]

There are some who theorize that crimes committed by blacks are "expressions of resistance."[29] In some measure, the disproportionate law-breaking by African Americans may be because they did not consent to the content of the law or to the way it is enforced. For those African Americans who are young and poor and answer questions about the future with "if I grow up" instead of "when I grow up,"[30] they may simply be breaking "a social contract that was not of their making in the first place."[31] Racism creates a destructive, self-fulfilling consequence: "Blacks can never quite respect laws which have no respect for them. . . . [L]aws designed to protect white men are viewed as white men's law."[32]

There is also no question that the extreme poverty of a substantial part of the African American community plays a role in the disproportionate numbers of blacks in the criminal system.[33] The Kerner Commission recognized this twenty-five years ago when it concluded that inner-city violence was a direct response to poverty, frustration, and neglect.[34] The commission warned that unless steps were taken to give poor African Americans a chance to participate in mainstream society, a permanent black underclass would be created, and it would be a continuing source of violent street crime.[35] In the 1990s, black children are almost three times as likely as white children to grow up in poor surroundings: 44.8% of black children live below the poverty line, compared with 15.9% of white youngsters.[36]

The truth is that most white Americans cannot begin to fathom the deprivation that many African Americans endure. To the middle-class whites in Simi Valley who exonerated the police officers in the first Rodney King trial, who refused to see what their eyes took in, the inner city is someplace to drive through only if there is no alternative, and only after locking the car doors. To the poverty-stricken residents of our nation's ghettos, who live without adequate food, housing, medical care, jobs, education, clean air, and physical safety, America's pledge of "liberty and justice for all" has long been broken. For the children, there is very little life at all:

> In one public housing project in Chicago, children play funeral: "They . . . build a casket with blocks and take turns lying in the casket. The children [take] on roles of preacher, family members, and mourners. They . . . weep and cry out for the person who died, saying, 'Don't take him!' "[37]

This country's ghettos contain and marginalize disproportionate numbers of poor African Americans (along with a seemingly anomalous underclass of white poor).[38] The ghettos are centers of drug addiction, AIDS, family violence, street crime, death, despair. Here, the harsh combination of race and poverty leaves an indelible mark: a man in Harlem is less likely to reach sixty-five than someone living in Bangladesh; black men are three times more likely to die of AIDS than whites; black men are seven times more likely to be murder victims than whites; black people are more likely to suffer from insomnia, obesity, and hypertension than whites.[39]

These are the people who are the most policed in our society. They are the children who grow up with nothing, believing they are nobody, who know more police officers than teachers and who have been in more jail cells than library carrels. They are the men and women humiliated by joblessness, homelessness, and their own powerlessness to change their lives. We police them to control them, to keep them in their place. One can only wonder what the world would look like if we took care of them instead.

It is in this wretched setting that most urban police officers function. It is hard, depressing, ceaseless work. There are many police officers who do it with compassion and connection. These men and women are the future of the American police. There are other police officers who, like a special militia for the commander in chief, carry out the War on Crime, the War on Drugs, and the War on Gangs against the entire minority community. These officers—and sometimes entire police forces— are occupiers,[40] not agents of justice.

The forces of racism and police militarism combine to dehumanize African American citizens; this, in turn, leads to a pattern of using excessive force against blacks and to beatings like that of Rodney King. Blacks are seen as the enemy, an enemy that is not quite flesh and blood like other people. There is little else that explains how "three baseball teams worth of cops" could have taken "batting practice on King's black body."[41] There is little else that explains how twelve jurors in the first trial could find no criminal wrongdoing. There is little else that explains the almost commonplace occurrence of police brutality against African Americans in cities all over this country.

Every other specific recommendation for change pales in comparison to acknowledging and addressing the ways in which racism informs every aspect of policing in this society. The police must stop doing the dirty work of the white power structure.[42] The police must stop being a force to keep black people down. Finally, the police must grapple with their fear of difference; they must discover that "them" and "us" are not very different at all.[43]

A change in the role of the police, without other social and political change, may not alter the nature of race relations in the United States. But would it not be wonderful if the police took a leadership role in reversing this nation's history of racism?

E   The Socialization of Police Officers

Much has been written about police culture.[44] Central to that culture are a number of widely held beliefs, among which are the following:

1   Police officers are the only real crime fighters.
2   Crime fighting is the central task of police officers.
3   No one else understands the true nature of police work. No one outside police departments—academics, politicians, and, especially, lawyers—can understand what

police officers have to do. The public is particularly naive.

4   Loyalty to other police officers—especially the rank and file—counts above everything else. Police officers must stick together. Everyone else is out to make policing difficult.

5   Police officers have to bend the rules in order to win the war against crime. The various rules that are supposed to protect individuals from police overreaching get in the way of effective law enforcement and allow the guilty to go free.

6   The police cannot count on public support. The public is unreasonably demanding and critical of police officers. The police are often blamed—and easily scapegoated—when something goes wrong.

7   Patrol work is a demeaning assignment, the lowest possible duty for a police officer. Only detectives and other specialists tackle serious crime issues.

8   "Problem-oriented policing," or "community policing," is for police officers who should have been social workers instead.

9   Though there are African Americans and other minorities who are *not* criminals, the truth is many are. There *is* such a thing as a criminal profile—which minority males often fit—and good police officers recognize it when they see it.

10   Force is the best way to establish authority in most situations on the street.[45]

An example of how police culture is drilled into officers as part of their orientation to police work was shared by a former police officer at the Miami hearings. Midgaly Rivas described a field-training assignment in 1990 during which she and other officers encountered an African American man who suddenly began shouting at them. While the other officers looked on, Rivas subdued the man by using the "minimum amount of force [required] to make him stop and listen"—her flashlight and her hands.[46]

A senior officer on the scene was angry that Rivas did not employ greater force and told her to do so. Rivas refused and continued to instruct the man verbally. At this point, the senior officer told him to leave—it turned out the man was often used by the police to "break in" female officers. Her superior then berated Rivas in front of the other officers for not following orders.[47]

Some of these core police beliefs contain some truth. The general public is not well informed about the real nature of police work and has an unrealistic expectation that police officers can control crime. The complex problems that underlie crime and the limited resources available to police make the task of crime control increasingly difficult. Police officers—even those who recognize the justification for constitutional constraints on their investigation and interrogation techniques—do feel hampered by "rules," and they sometimes resort to "cheating" to ensure the right result. The experience of police officers may well be that force is a useful tool, that large numbers of minority males are arrested and charged with crime, and that patrol work (whether it be called "community policing" or some other trendy phrase) is depressing.

Still, these beliefs encourage police behavior that ranges from the insensitive to the brutal and that promotes institutional insularity and detachment. Replacing these beliefs with more productive values must be at the heart of any reform strategy.[48]

FINDINGS

A Racism Is a Central Part of Police Misconduct

1 Finding: Race is a chief motivating factor in police suspicion, investigation, and stops and searches

Racism critically influences how the police perform their law-enforcement functions. The use of sweeps through minority areas in the name of crime fighting,[1] the targeting of young black males for "stop and frisks,"[2] the targeting of young black males for humiliating strip searches, even in public,[3] and the creation of criminal profiles that inevitably focus on African Americans and Latinos[4] have become standard police practice in urban America. Rarely does one find the same extreme measures taking place in white areas, notwithstanding the fact that crime occurs there too.

In testimony at the Norfolk, Virginia, hearing, attorney Bernard T. Holmes relayed a revealing incident about policing in the context of both race and gender. He received a call from the mother of a sixteen-year-old black girl. The teenager had been at a carnival with a white girl of the same age and two young black men. They left the carnival and were approached by police officers as they sat necking in their car at two o'clock in the morning. The police insisted that the white girl be taken to the station to be picked up by her parents and left the black girl on the street. The officers ignored the pleas of the black girl to take her with them and to not separate her from her girlfriend. The mother of the black girl felt that the "integrity and virginity" of the black girl was not considered as important by the police as that of the white girl.[5]

Professor Andrew Cherry of Barry University described racially based harassment and arrests of particularly vulnerable African Americans in the Miami area. Noting that African Americans there constitute an increasingly large majority of the homeless (67 percent in 1991),[6] Cherry gave numerous examples of how police harassment "makes it more and more difficult for the homeless to get off the streets."[7] For example, on a daily basis police round up car-window washers, whose ranks are predominantly or entirely black and who have no other employment. The police take them to the station, book them, hold them—without food, without allowing them to sleep or to bathe—and then return them to their original locations.

Police officers have gone into parks as they are about to open in the morning and have confiscated, and sometimes burned, the belongings of the homeless, including identification. People are thus forced to move from area to area. The police have driven into parks where the homeless are sleeping, turned on their lights and sirens, and announced over loudspeakers, "[I]t is 2:00 A.M. in the morning and it is raining."[8] Police also conduct prostitution stings in areas frequented by the homeless, offering money to women: "[I]t is almost inevitably a black lady, they will offer her money that she, virtually, cannot resist. Then they arrest the person."[9]

Professor Cherry, who has been studying the homeless in the Miami area for several years, testified that there were no black police officers working with this population. He stated he had witnessed more than a dozen cases of harassment of homeless people but had only once seen the police arrest a white homeless person. He described the response to a confrontation between two homeless men—one white, one black. Arriving on the scene of the incident, Barry saw the black man in the patrol car and the white man outside the car talking to the officers, despite the fact that it turned out that it was the white man who had pulled out a weapon.[10]

At the time of the NAACP hearings in Miami, the ACLU had brought suit against the City of Miami and the Miami Police Department, challenging the police practice of confiscating and trashing the possessions of the homeless.[11] Professor Cherry testified that all of the plaintiffs in the ACLU suit were African Americans.[12]

Police officers have increasingly come to rely on race as the primary indicator of both suspicious conduct and dangerousness. There is a long-standing feeling in the black community, based on police practices, that the police regard all community members as either criminals or potential criminals. As one scholar of police conduct noted, "There is substantial evidence that many police officers believe minority race indicates a general propensity to commit crime."[13]

By law, the police may not stop people on the street without cause.[14] Twenty-five years ago, in *Terry v. Ohio*,[15] the United States Supreme Court recognized that the power to stop people and to conduct an outer-body frisk, considered a lesser intrusion than a full-fledged search, could be used to harass minorities. Sounding eerily prescient, the Court referred to police practices that "can only serve to exacerbate police-community tensions in the crowded centers of our nation's cities."

In *Terry*, Chief Justice Warren quoted at length from a report of the President's Commission on Law Enforcement and the Administration of Justice, which concluded that field interrogations and "stop and frisks" are a major source of friction between the police and minority groups. According to the report, much of the tension related to the officers' "perceived need to maintain the power image of the beat officer, an aim sometimes accomplished by humiliating anyone who attempts to undermine police control of the streets."[16]

In practice, however, *Terry*—which requires that police, in order to perform a stop and frisk, have an objective, articulable suspicion that a suspect has been involved in a crime and a reasonable belief that the suspect is armed and dangerous—has little force. In the context of drugs, guns, and the popular perception of a crime epidemic, the mere status of being a minority-group member in a poor urban area has come to justify a *Terry* stop. As police officer Ernie Neal stated at the Miami hearings after commenting upon the fact that African Americans and other minorities are much more likely to be arrested than whites—"[A]n arrest is a discretionary situation which may have a lifetime impact upon a person whose major offense was that he was not sufficiently respectful or deferential toward the police."[17]

Police officers have come to realize that several factors are working in their favor when they stop people without sufficient cause: usually, those stopped do not make formal complaints; an allegation by the suspect of an illegal stop will generally only occur in a motion to suppress evidence, filed by the suspect as part of his or her defense to a criminal prosecution; the state's burden of proof in such a motion is slight—a mere preponderance of the evidence; the motion will boil down to the police officer's word against that of the suspect; the allegation will likely go no further if there was no evidence of physical violence by the arresting officer.

Unfortunately, the evisceration of the Fourth Amendment in minority neighborhoods is not solely a police tactic. Joining police and law-enforcement officials in the disembowelment of the right (of black people) to be free from unreasonable searches and seizures are prosecutors, judges, the press, politicians, and some members of minority communities. The ravages of drugs and crime have made for strange bedfellows. Minority-community members who are willing to tolerate improper, intrusive police behavior do so for the promise of a safer neighborhood.[18]

As young black people have come to know well, however, there is a cost. Studies have shown that young African Americans are more likely to be suspected of crime than other groups and that deadly force is more readily used against black suspects.[19] One out of every four black men between the ages of twenty and twenty-nine is either on probation, on parole, or in jail.[20]

Even in nonthreatening situations, minorities often find themselves harassed by the police. There was testimony at the Miami hearings that in one Dade County mall there is a policy of stopping black youths to ask if they have money. If they do not, they are ejected from the mall.[21] This is a frequent occurrence in Boston-area shopping malls, where young black men are stopped if they are "not shopping" and evicted. If they return, they are arrested for trespass.[22]

Ours is a deeply racist society, and it is important to note that the police are not the only source of race-based suspicion. During the Indianapolis hearings, Joseph Johnson recounted a harrowing experience at the hands of the Indiana University/

Purdue University police and Indianapolis police, prompted by a university librarian who had contacted police because Mr. Johnson had "left the library at 10 o'clock on five consecutive nights without a book [under] his arm."[23] Mr. Johnson, an African American alumnus of the university, had been conducting research from books on *reserve,* which could not be taken out of the library.[24] Mr. Johnson testified that after he left the library building, he heard a voice say, "Hey, you. I want to talk to you."[25] Turning around, he saw only blinding headlights. When he continued to walk away, an unknown person grabbed his arm. Running to escape from what he thought were would-be muggers, Mr. Johnson was stopped by officers in four police cars, with clubs and guns drawn.[26] He was "hit twice with billy clubs . . . lifted . . . up off the concrete, raised . . . in the air, . . . and body slammed . . . on the hood of the . . . car."[27] The police charged him with resisting arrest and took him to jail.[28]

2 Finding: Young black men are overrepresented in the criminal justice system

Mary Redd, of the Norfolk Urban League, observed that "there are some officers who see . . . behind practically every African American male face . . . a gang member, behind every African American teenage face a threat. . . ."[29] With this police perspective as a backdrop, it is not surprising that in April 1991 the National Center on Institutions and Alternatives found that in Washington, D.C., on any given day, 42 percent of black men between the ages of eighteen and thirty-five were enmeshed in the criminal justice system. They were either in jail, on probation, on parole, out on bond, or being sought on an arrest warrant. The same organization, in a recent study of Baltimore, found that, on any given day, 56 percent of the city's young black men aged eighteen to thirty-five were somehow caught up in the criminal justice system. A great many of the arrests made in Baltimore last year—thirteen thousand of them—were related to drug charges; of those arrested, eleven thousand (85 percent) were black. This is a stunning figure. The National Institute on Drug Abuse estimates that 77 percent of all drug users in this country are white.[30] Note who's being arrested.[31]

Billy Murphy, a Baltimore attorney, says that the explanation for these extraordinary numbers is simple. "Getting tough on crime, first of all, is a buzzword for 'Let's get the niggers,' and 'Let's get the Latinos.' Because we all know, the conventional wisdom says, that they are the cause of our problem, they are making our society more violent, they are reducing the quality of our life."[32] So the war on crime becomes a war on people of color, largely those who are young and male.

For all the attention being paid to young African American men by the police, there seem to be relatively few cases of members of this population posing a direct, serious threat to them. Few are alleged to have shot at or killed police officers, for example. George E. Mins, president of the Virginia Beach NAACP, testified that he could think of only one instance where a young black man's actions resulted in the killing of a police officer in the Virginia Beach area.[33] Yet the police there tend to focus on, and to come down harder on, this particular group.

The question then becomes why, in the context of drugs, the police treat young black men differently from the way they treat anyone else. Young white men sell drugs, and young whites use drugs, but there is not the same level of police hostility. The only difference is race.[34]

As a result of what they experience at the hands of the police, there is a growing perception among young African American men that they are not being treated fairly. Bernard T. Holmes testified that as an attorney he gets numerous calls from young black men who complain about the treatment they receive at the hands of the police.[35] They can be future doctors and lawyers (and police officers), but many police still see them as suspects, drug dealers, and gang members—they are all too often "Presumed Guilty."[36]

Young black men have come to experience police stops, questioning, and harassment as their American way of life. This may be especially true for black men on American highways. Casey Stuart is a thirty-two-year-old black man. "I've been driving since I was 14. Being stopped is something that's part of life out here [Los Angeles]. That's life."[37] The constitutional protections he learned about in civics class apparently apply to others, not him.

Interviewed for a television news program, Los Angeles Police Chief Willie Williams stated, "I think that African American males and other minority males are more prone to be stopped for small or frivolous reasons than non–African American males in not just big cities like Los Angeles and Philadelphia, but small, suburban and rural and country towns. Statistically, it is a fact."[38]

Brian Bowens, on the same television news program, put it plainly: "I'm six feet five and a half, I'm dark-skinned, I'm black. You know, if I have dark glasses on, a baseball cap, it fits a profile, why not be afraid? That's what white America says, right? But if I'm a white guy driving around in a Benz, talking on a car phone, listening to loud music, he goes on. 'Oh what a businessman, an executive, movie star, whatever.' When I'm doing it, 'drug dealer.' "[39]

A member of the Urban League in the Norfolk area testified that she witnessed a white officer stop a young, "clean-cut, clean-shaven" black Norfolk State University student, allegedly for making an illegal turn on his bicycle, then bang him against the police car and detain him for an hour and a half. When she spoke with the young man after the incident, he said the officer told him that "you can go down and file a complaint about the police brutality if you want to, but I just beat two raps on that. . . ."

She subsequently found out that the officer had indeed just "beaten" a couple of cases with internal affairs. She testified that when she called someone in the police administration, she was told:

> [W]hat you don't understand . . . is that some Jamaicans have been out here shooting at night and they thought it was a problem. I said, wait a minute. They couldn't have thought that. The kid had no gun. The kid had nothing. That doesn't justify it because we do have a problem with gangs in the projects. That doesn't justify treating this kid that way.[40]

B Citizens Experience Police Abuse in a Wide Variety of Forms

1 Finding: Excessive force has become a standard part of the arrest procedure

Perhaps the most serious problem facing the minority community is police use of excessive and deadly force in the name of law enforcement. Excessive force encompasses everything from brutal beatings to the use of police dogs to police shootings. Citizens testified about the brutality employed in many routine arrests. Even when a suspect has demonstrated an intention to surrender, physical punishment is frequently a part of the arrest process.

Public defenders, criminal defense lawyers, and criminal clinicians in law schools (including some of the authors of this book) routinely hear descriptions of excessive force when clients recount the way in which they were arrested. Sometimes it seems that criminal suspects who are *not* handcuffed too tightly, *not* smacked with a nightstick, and *not* shoved into a police wagon are the exception.

Recently, one of the authors of this book represented a client accused of participating in a melee where rocks were thrown. The client, a seventeen-year-old high school student, captain of the track team and college bound, was walking home after a party in a church when he was stopped by police officers and ordered to the ground. The student complied and, on his own, got into a "spread eagle" position. While he lay there in a state of complete surrender, a police officer came up from behind and kicked him hard between the legs. The same officer then hit the student in the back of the head with a flashlight. He threatened worse if the young man moved.

The student had no intention of doing anything other than what he had been ordered to do. He wanted no trouble. He had never been in any trouble. He had been taught to respect and heed police officers. He had done nothing wrong, and he believed that once the police determined that they had the wrong person he would be free to go. Instead, he was assaulted and then arrested. The police allege that the young man threw rocks at them. He was subsequently tried for assault and battery with a dangerous weapon and found not guilty.

Glenn Stewart's story is a nightmarish part of the same picture. A Miami resident, he was pulled over for reckless driving and not stopping for a police officer. When he got out of his car, the Metro-Dade police officer "was spinning [him] around handcuffed" and delivered a "whack on the back of [his] neck." This blow caused him to suffer a broken neck, which resulted in paralysis. He spent three months in the hospital and required spinal cord surgery.[41]

Many law-enforcement officers testified that the problem of excessive force has diminished somewhat due to an effort on the part of police departments to rid themselves of troubled personnel. For example, former Indianapolis Chief of Police Paul Anee pointed out that police shootings in Indianapolis have fallen steadily in recent years. According to Chief Anee, there were 29 "police action shootings," including 12 fatalities, in 1974, and 27 shootings, including 7 fatalities, in 1975. In contrast, there were 3 police shootings (1 fatality) in 1986, 2 police shootings (1 fatality) in 1987, 3 police shootings (1 fatality) in 1988, 6 police shootings (3 fatalities) in 1989, and 8 police shootings (3 fatalities) in 1990.[42]

Maj. Sheldon Darden, chief of operations for the Norfolk Police Department, pointed out that his department has a policy that does not allow officers "to tolerate police brutality, excessive use of force and the abuse of police authority." He said that it is important to strictly enforce this policy.[43] The vice-mayor of Norfolk testified that of seventy deaths reported in the city in 1990, none was related to police misconduct or intervention.[44]

In Signal Hill, Los Angeles County, Chief Michael McCrary

echoed the sentiments of Major Darden. He testified that one of the first announcements he made to officers under his command after taking control of that city's police department was that police misconduct was not acceptable.

> Excessive force would not be tolerated. I clearly told them the expectation was they were to do their job. At times we deal with people and we're going to have to use force, they are to use force but nothing excessive. . . . Any excessive force would be fully investigated. Any violations would result in termination. . . . We found they could do their jobs without use of excessive force, so that was not a problem.[45]

Still, excessive force remains a problem throughout the country, especially as it involves minorities. The police in the Miami/Metro-Dade area, for example, have a long history of such conduct. At a forum conducted by the Florida Advisory Committee to the United States Commission on Civil Rights in 1988, a community organization presented accounts of the killing or beating of fifteen blacks under "cloudy circumstances" in Dade County since 1979. At the time of the forum, the state's attorney's office listed seventeen "questionable" cases of the use of deadly force, going back to 1986.[46]

At the NAACP hearings in Miami, People United to Lead the Struggle for Equality (PULSE)—a community organization that participated in the 1988 Florida Advisory Committee forum—presented a list of police beatings and shootings. It included seven incidents in which black people had been shot under suspicious circumstances between 1979 and 1988 in the Miami/Metro-Dade area. In the same record, PULSE documented eight brutal beatings,[47] including the beating deaths of

Arthur McDuffie and Randolph McFadden. McDuffie, an African American insurance executive, was beaten to death on December 17, 1979; McFadden died while in police custody on January 11, 1988, under suspicious circumstances.[48]

Despite a growing national reputation for excessively violent police behavior, Miami and Metro-Dade police continue to use force, especially against minorities. The Miami-Dade Branch of the NAACP documented twenty-one complaints of police misconduct and abuse between January 1990 and August 1991, eleven of which involved unnecessary or excessive physical violence.[49] In 1991, Metro-Dade officers "arrested and physically abused a black male clothing concession owner after the concession owner asked the officers why they were harassing his customers."[50] Also in 1991, Miami Beach officers beat an African American man who insisted he had not committed a crime. The citizen was stripped naked, cuffed hand and foot, thrown in a chilly jail cell, and charged only with resisting arrest.[51]

In Los Angeles, attorney Johnny L. Cochran testified about excessive force in his city:

> Mr. Darryl Stephens was a young man 27 years of age. A young man who was in bed in a residence out here in El Monte. El Monte is an area just east of Los Angeles. This is not a Sheriff's case. I believe this is an El Monte Police case. The SWAT squad comes into this man's house in the early hours, apparently looking for suspects or weapons that were used by some people who had been kidnapping people from a mall. This man is laying [sic] in his bed, apparently on his stomach. Coroner's report is out today. He was shot 28 times in the back.[52]

Henry Paxton, another attorney, told about the death of a second Los Angeles citizen. On November 29, 1991, at approximately 5:50 P.M., twenty-seven-year-old Henry Peco III was walking to a gym in Los Angeles to pick up several children and take them home. As he was walking to the gym, Mr. Peco passed his sister and his cousin. Within seconds repeated gunfire was heard. His cousin saw someone fall and began to scream, "No, not him." Mr. Peco's sister immediately ran to his assistance.

While she was trying to revive him, the sister was threatened by uniformed officers from the South Central Division of the Los Angeles Police Department. "They put a gun to her head and told her to move, that she was interfering with police work."[53] The officers pulled her off her brother, and they then pulled off two of his cousins who had come to his aid and arrested them.

Mr. Peco died of "numerous gunshot wounds." Although the police apparently claimed that he had a rifle, no weapon was ever found.[54]

On October 31, 1989, in Houston, three drunk, off-duty police officers chased a fifty-year-old black woman for thirteen miles on a Texas freeway before shooting her to death. The officers apparently became enraged when Mrs. Ida Lee Delaney, who was on her way to work in the early morning, cut them off. None of the officers was in uniform, and they were driving a private, unmarked car as they chased Mrs. Delaney. In fear of her unknown pursuers, she fired shots at their car before pulling over. One officer approached the car and exchanged fire, leaving himself wounded and Mrs. Delaney dead. The officer was found to have a blood alcohol level of nearly twice the legal limit. He was subsequently convicted of manslaughter.[55]

The increased use of police dogs is another example of the

trend toward excessive force in minority communities. At the Los Angeles hearings, there was testimony about the employment of police dogs to punish those who attempt to run from officers.

Attorney Donald W. Cook testified that it is "the practice of virtually every police agency in southern California to use the dogs to attack people whenever the dog finds the person [who has run], irrespective of what the person is doing." The dogs, seventy- to eighty-pound German shepherds, are trained to attack "as hard as the dog can" and to make "full mouth bites, meaning to get the entire jaw wrapped around whatever part of the body it can bite, and to bite down as hard as it can for as long as it can."[56] If the suspect breaks free, the dog "bite[s] again and again and again."[57] The dog will stop only when the handler pulls it off, which usually does not happen until the suspect "becomes still."[59]

Mr. Cook testified that dogs are used primarily in investigations of property crimes like burglaries and thefts. These crimes occur "a little more frequently" in the wealthier, white neighborhoods of Los Angeles, yet these communities have the least number of dog-bite incidents. He went on to point out that the number of dog-bite incidents is disproportionately high in the African American and Latino communities. In Los Angeles, most officers with dogs patrol the South Central district. The rationale that "the dogs go where the crimes are" or that a higher violent crime rate justifies the use of dogs is not true: LAPD statistics show a lower than average use-of-force rate in the public division that generates the highest number of dog bites—a primarily African American area.[59]

What is most disturbing is that many victims of dog bites are accused of nonviolent crimes and pose no immediate threat to the police or civilians.[60] The *Seattle Times* reported an incident in Tacoma in which four men were accused of stealing a car; police dogs were brought to the scene and unleashed, even though the men appeared to be unarmed.[61]

In Los Angeles, Fernandez Hernandez, under arrest for drunk driving and car theft, was taken to San Clemente General Hospital for treatment of dog bites on both thighs. The incident began when the California Highway Patrol pursued Mr. Hernandez south on Interstate 5 in the Mission Viejo area because his license plate indicated the car was stolen. During the pursuit, Hernandez suddenly stopped, got out of the car, and ran across the freeway lanes into a large field. The California Highway Patrol searched the field, assisted by helicopters. Using infrared sensors that detected the suspect's body heat in the tall, dense brush, the police found their man—and sent in Nick, a German shepherd police dog with the sheriff's department.[62]

The Philadelphia Police Department has the distinction of having the greatest number of police dogs, with approximately twice as many dogs as Los Angeles. However, while there have been about nine hundred attacks by police dogs in a three-year period in Los Angeles, there were only twenty dog bites during the same period in Philadelphia.[63]

2   Finding: Physical abuse by police officers is not unusual or aberrational

At the Indianapolis hearings, Selvei Burris testified that the police came into his house and arrested his whole family, beating and kicking them in the process. He was removed from his home and taken to the police station, where he was held overnight before being released.[64]

They [four police officers] came to our house. My son has a girl-friend. . . . I allowed them to stay at my house. . . . Well, the police, the girl's father and mother came. And when they came they came in with four police officers. During this time as they entered the house I went in behind them and I asked them what was the prob-lem. And they asked me to leave, which I told him—I said, "It's my house, I would like to know what's going on." At the time they told me that they were investigating that the girl had been held against her will. And I said, "Well, she is sitting there. And all you had to do is ask if she's being held against her will." Well, next thing I know . . . my daughter, my son, my wife and I all four were arrested. My wife was brutalized, my son was brutalized, my daughter was brutalized. . . . And the officer grabbed me, spun me around. . . . [A] young man kicked me. He kicked me the second time. Then he started choking me.[65]

Though no one in the household did more than ask the po-lice what they wanted, the officers seemed to regard them all as criminals before they even entered the home. The physical abuse that followed was an unnecessary control technique that had nothing to do with law enforcement and everything to do with race.[66]

Nor will station in life shield one from excessive police intru-sion. Black professionals are as likely to be victims of police misconduct as the less affluent. For example, on June 6, 1988, Metro-Dade police officers went to a black household in which the father was a tenured professor and the mother an accoun-tant. Their thirteen-year-old daughter had called her uncle about a verbal dispute between her parents. The uncle called the police, who came long after the argument had ceased. They entered the house, struck the father with a club, and then at-tacked the mother when she tried to protect her husband. The father was beaten to unconsciousness while handcuffed; his injuries included lacerations, contusions, and fractured ribs. The wife required two surgeries for knee injuries. Police also struck the daughter with a club, resulting in thirteen stitches to her head. Though there was no evidence of criminal conduct on the part of anyone, the police assaulted all those in the house. Both parents were charged with assaulting officers and resisting arrest; they were eventually acquitted by a jury.[67]

Jody Lee, a young African American man in Indianapolis, testified that he was removed from his house and beaten as a means of interrogation.

> I was taken out of my home by a police officer and he said I was going to be arrested. And I was placed under arrest, which I was outside of my door. The officer took me out to the car, placed me in the vehicle, drove me across the street to a parking lot, asked me some questions about something that had happened. I told him I didn't know the people['s] names that were involved. The officer took me out of the car. . . . Then once they got me out, they threw me on the ground and started to hit on me, and kick me, and things. They hit me with the night sticks. The officer went back to his car and got a stun gun out and he had me on the ground and shot me with the stun gun. This whole time this happened I was handcuffed behind my back. Then they handcuffed my hands and legs together and one officer stood in the middle of my back with his foot. . . . All those officers were white. One of them had me on the ground, another one said to another officer, "I ought to put a bullet in his head."[68]

Mr. Lee was charged with resisting arrest, public intoxication, and battery.[69]

On June 21, 1991, in North Miami Beach, Willie Mitchell's

grandson was bringing his car home after it had been repaired. He was stopped by police, who claimed the car had been involved in a burglary, despite the fact that it had been garaged for two months. Notified of the mistake, Mr. Mitchell went to the scene and told officers that the vehicle had in fact been in the garage for repairs. The car was impounded by the police and investigated; eventually, it was determined that the car had not been involved in any illegal activity. Mr. Mitchell's son then drove it home.

When he arrived, an armed police officer was waiting in an unmarked police car. He jumped out of his car and pursued Mr. Mitchell's son to the house, where he kicked in the front door. The officer subsequently said that he was going to arrest the son and "tow that mother-fucking car in." Other police officers came to the scene. Once inside the house, four policemen held the son on the floor while the first officer choked him. Other officers threw the owner of the car, his wife, and his daughter on the floor or against a wall, arresting him, his son, and his daughter.

The son was charged with assault, intimidating an officer, and resisting arrest; the other family members were charged with obstruction of justice. The Mitchells testified that they are the third black family in their neighborhood whose front door has been kicked in by police officers.[70]

3   Finding: Verbal abuse and harassment are the most common forms of police abuse and are standard police behavior in minority communities

Police were consistently found to use verbal abuse, disrespectful conduct, and harassment in all types of encounters. This was the most frequent complaint about police officers in the various cities. Verbal abuse and harassment seem to occur almost every time a minority citizen is stopped by a police officer. However, its occurrence is also vastly underreported. If the person is released after such an encounter, there is little incentive after the initial anger has passed to pursue a complaint against the police. If the person is charged with a criminal offense, she or he must defend against the perception that she or he is a criminal and is saying anything against the police to "get over."

The testimony presented strongly suggests that, for the minority community, verbal abuse and harassment by the police are standard operating procedure. There appears to be little distinction between the type of abuse and harassment by the authorities that people of color experience on the street and in their homes.[71]

Carl Kelley testified about an incident that occurred in his house in Indianapolis on December 14, 1990. A black man attempted to come into Mr. Kelley's home without identifying himself, looking for someone that Mr. Kelley did not know. Kelley stopped the man before he could get into the house and told him that the person he was looking for did not live there. It turned out the black man was an undercover police officer. Once he and a uniformed officer entered, they insisted on being shown identification and delivered a lecture to Mr. Kelley about his parenting responsibilities. They then left, without an explanation or apology.[72]

James Foster, a lawyer, testified about the utter disregard the Los Angeles County Sheriff's department has for area residents. On September 26, 1991, fourteen attorneys filed a class-action complaint in the federal district court on behalf of seventy-five victims of police misconduct.[73] The complaint alleged "systematic lawlessness and wanton abuse of power and widespread harassment by Sheriff's deputies of the Lynwood station."

> The complaint, "Darren Thomas, et al. against the County of Los Angeles," described 130 abusive acts, almost exclusively against African Americans and Latinos, consisting of unjustified shootings, beatings, killings and destruction of property by Lynwood deputy sheriffs within a span of 104 days. . . . These acts included at least 69 warrantless harassing arrests and detentions . . . 31 incidents of excessive force and unwarranted abuse against handcuffed and otherwise defenseless detainees, and consisted of kicking, pushing, striking with flashlights, choking, slamming doors on legs, seven ransackings of homes and businesses, sixteen incidents of outright torture, meaning interrogations with stun guns, beating victims into unconsciousness, holding a gun in a victim's mouth and pulling the trigger on an empty chamber, quick stop driving to bang a victim's head against the screen and epithets by deputies such as niggers and wetbacks.[74]

Most of this "terrorism," according to Mr. Foster, was caused by a white supremacist group of deputies, called the Vikings, based in the Lynwood substation; it often occurred when the police claimed to be looking for drugs. "[W]hat they usually do . . . [is] rouse the whole family and put them outside in their underwear, and go in, usually without a search warrant and trash the house with the excuse that they are gang members."[75]

Individual or small-group racist behavior, however, cannot account for such thoroughgoing misconduct as that documented by the Lynwood Litigation Team. Such massive destruction and excessive behavior, in so short a period, implicates not only those officers directly involved but the hierarchy of the police department as well.

In Miami, David Perkins testified that a crowd had gathered at the scene of an apparent robbery and homicide. The police already had the area roped off and were in control of the situation. For some reason, officers came into the crowd and began beating up a young woman. When others in the crowd complained, the police left the woman to beat up a young man. Rocks and bottles were thrown at the police, who brought in twenty to thirty more officers with tear gas and guns. When Mr. Perkins asked to speak to a police sergeant on the scene, he was told, "Nigger, get back across the street or else your ass [is] going to jail."[76]

On another occasion, a retired U.S. Army sergeant, Alexander Kelly, was watching a nonviolent Haitian demonstration in Miami when he was accosted by police officers. While he was being held by the police, one of them said to him, "Oh, you['re] old enough to remember when we used to beat the shit out of niggers. I want you to stand here, watch how we beat these niggers out there."[77]

4   Finding: False charges and retaliatory actions against abused citizens sometimes follow incidents of abuse

Often, police misconduct does not end with physical violence or verbal abuse. Far too frequently, the citizen who has just been subjected to police abuse is then arrested and charged with a variety of crimes. The most common charges are disorderly conduct, resisting arrest, and assaulting a police officer. George E. Mins, the president of the Virginia Beach NAACP, testified that resisting-arrest charges are "excessively used, unnecessarily used, and very often in cases where there was some questionable conduct on the part of the officer."[78]

Norfolk attorney William P. Robinson testified that misdemeanor charges inevitably follow a confrontation with police officers. Often these charges lead to mandatory jail time.[79] Many judges find any allegation of assault on a police officer, frequently made in these circumstances, particularly egregious and are likely to sentence persons so charged more harshly.

While there are no distinct lines separating charges with some basis from those with none, there are some factual patterns that indicate the latter. Routine stops that escalate into charges against the citizen are a common problematic event. Another is the case of a citizen charged with assaulting an officer, even though the citizen is injured and the officer is not.[80]

Some citizens are charged with offenses because they complain about treatment at the hands of police. Such charges serve to justify the force used by the officers and the injuries done to the person arrested, as well as providing leverage and bargaining power. Many district attorneys will dismiss charges upon waiver of civil litigation against the police officer or the police department.[81]

Sometimes innocent bystanders end up as criminal defendants. Here is the experience of a witness to police abuse in the Los Angeles area.

On November the 26th, 1991, the Sheriff's Department of Lynwood responded to a call at my neighbor's house. I heard some noises outside the window. I got up, looked out the window. It was after 8 P.M. . . . . I was asleep. I heard a female voice and a male voice, and I saw a Sheriff deputy hit my neighbor . . . with a club. I went outside and confronted two Sheriff's deputies. [My neighbor] was handcuffed while the deputy hit him on his back. I asked, "Why are you beating the man." The deputy said, "Get out of our way. Let us do our job," in foul language. Immediately after, I was pushed two times by the deputy. I begged the deputy again to stop beating him. While they had [my neighbor] down more Sheriff deputies came up. One of the Sheriff deputies that came up asked me what happened. When I mentioned to him that I saw the deputy beat this man, he immediately grabbed me, threw my hands behind me, handcuffed me and dragged me over to the car and took me off to jail, charged me with obstructing a peace officer and battery, which I never laid a hand on the deputy.[82]

C Police Departments Have Only Begun to Address Police Abuse and Have Failed to Track or Discipline Officers Who Are Repeat Offenders

1 Finding: Some police departments have established new policies regarding the use of force against citizens

Representatives of several police departments testified that they had adopted specific policies and procedures to regulate the use of force. Representatives from the Miami, Metro-Dade, Houston, Virginia Beach, and Chesapeake, Virginia, police departments testified that their revised deadly force policies authorized the use of deadly force in fewer circumstances than those defined by the laws of their states.[83] According to these police officials, their new policies permit the use of deadly force only to protect the officer's life or that of another and/or to stop someone in the commission of a violent felony.[84] Chief Ross testified that in the Miami Police Department, police shootings that result in injury or death are open to immediate review by the homicide unit, internal affairs, the civilian review agency, the state attorney's office, the medical examiner's office, and various police officials.[85]

Some police and elected officials described new policies regarding the types of weapons or force that can be used by police officers. Mayor William Hudnut of Indianapolis endorsed the use of chemical repellents as an alternative to deadly force, a practice instituted by the outgoing chief of police.[86] The chief of the Chesapeake Police Department testified that he had revised the department's firearms policies to standardize both the type of weapon used in the department and training in that particular firearm. He also replaced electric-shock devices and most nonlethal gases with one chemical agent. Instead of being able to employ such weapons as billy clubs, slap sticks, and blackjacks, officers may use a "baton," but must pass a course before they are authorized to carry it.[87] The Long Beach Police Department established a new policy that requires an officer who applies a carotid-artery control ("choke hold") to take the person upon whom it is used to a medical doctor; as a result, the use of the control was significantly reduced.[88]

2 Finding: Many departments have inadequate procedures for monitoring and responding to patterns of misconduct by officers

Many police forces lack adequate systems for detecting patterns of misconduct by individual officers or for discerning the types of situations in which misconduct most frequently occurs. Citizens in several cities testified that the majority of the incidents of police brutality involve a minority of officers.[89] Some testified that the same officers engage in repeated acts of misconduct against citizens and are known within the police department,[90] yet the department fails to adequately discipline the officers who commit acts of brutality.[91] A Norfolk witness testified that the officers who have the problems "oftentimes are not sensitive to African Americans."[92] Many citizens and community groups voiced the need for effective monitoring and control of officers.[93]

Recent surveys of the use of force in particular police departments have found a concentration of complaints against certain officers, accompanied by a departmental failure to monitor and discipline them. The Christopher Commission Report notes a 1991 survey of excessive- or unnecessary-force complaints against Los Angeles police officers during a five and one-half year period. The survey found that 254 of the 1,931 officers complained of were named in three or more incident reports and represented 30 percent of the complaints; 47 officers had five or more complaints.[94] According to the Christopher Commission Report, although the problem officers are well known, they are not adequately disciplined. For example, many of the 88 officers who participated in a drug raid in 1988, in which "massive damage" was inflicted on homes and 127 acts of vandalism were carried out, had been promoted. Even an officer who had been disciplined for making false statements in a search warrant affidavit was promoted.[95] Although many of those with patterns of repeated use of force had "similar patterns" in previous years, which could not be fully explained by arrest rates or officer assignments, "no audit or review of patterns of use of force reports appears to have been made by the LAPD."[96] Even some high-ranking officers testified before the Christopher Commission that the LAPD has "failed miserably" in holding supervisors accountable for use of excessive force by officers under their command.[97]

A 1992 *Boston Globe* investigative series reported a "dramatic increase" in citizen complaints of abuse by officers in that city, from 33 in 1983 to 175 in 1990. The increase was "fueled in large part by a small number of officers."[98] Eleven percent of all officers were named in 61.5 percent of the complaints, while two-thirds of all officers had no abuse complaints. Five officers had been investigated by the internal affairs division of the Boston Police Department one hundred times between 1981 and 1990 on complaints ranging from harassment and verbal abuse to illegal search, false arrest, and physical abuse. The officers were cleared by internal affairs in ninety of the investigations and, for the most part, received mild reprimands in the remaining cases. All of the officers were still on the force in 1992.[99]

The St. Clair Commission had previously found a "disturbing pattern of violence toward citizens by a small number of officers in the Boston Police Department."[100] Its review of a sample of the internal affairs division complaints filed in 1989 and 1990 revealed that at least half of the officers complained of had been the subject of previous complaints.[101] Among this group, the median number of complaints was three.[102] Ten percent of the 134 officers with previous complaints in the sample cases had more than ten prior complaints.[103]

Witnesses at the NAACP hearings testified that the failure to adequately monitor, as well as train and supervise, officers can have disastrous consequences, a position supported by the

Christopher Commission.[104] For example, an attorney for the families of two African Americans fatally shot by Houston police in two separate incidents testified that the officer in each case had a history of misconduct that had been ignored. One of the officers had killed three black men in four years as a patrolman.[105] A representative of the Houston Police Department, Assistant Chief Jimmy L. Dotson, testified that had a recently established monitoring system been in place at the time of one of the shootings, the officer, who had a history of violent incidents, would have been "identified" and monitored.[106]

Some police departments have instituted procedures to establish quality control and to discern patterns of misconduct. The adequacy and scope of the quality control mechanisms varies greatly from department to department and ranges from personal oversight by the chief or upper-echelon officers to sophisticated review systems.

The Metro-Dade Police Department established an "early warning system" in late 1982. It provides systematic review of complaints and use-of-force incidents, with the aim of catching problems before they become a crisis.[107] Quarterly reports identify officers with two or more personnel complaints or involvement in three or more use-of-force incidents in the quarter; annual reports are also made.[108] These documents go to the employee's supervisor, who is required to make a detailed report, which is then reviewed by the department's Professional Compliance Bureau. Officers may be referred to psychological services or to a stress reduction program. Supervisors may impose "corrective" action: counseling, discipline, or termination.[109]

The Miami Police Department has a similar program whereby officers with a certain number of complaints within a three-month period are tracked and monitored. A sergeant, who is generally the first to receive and review complaints about an officer's conduct, counsels him or her individually. If the conduct persists, the officer can be referred to a consulting firm of psychologists for counseling and/or evaluation of fitness for duty. According to one of the consulting psychologists, the department usually tries to "treat mental disorders or even burnout . . . to allow that officer some opportunity for rehabilitation."[110] The consultant also testified that it was common for officers to be taken off the streets and assigned to desk duty while they participate in counseling. Officers may be relieved from duty with pay, contingent upon participation in treatment. Generally, a liaison monitors the case to ensure compliance by the officer. Those who refuse to comply with orders for evaluation or counseling face disciplinary action, ranging from suspension to dismissal.[111]

In April 1990 the Houston Police Department instituted the Personnel Concerns Program for officers with a "pattern of complaints . . . [that] cause concern."[112] Houston's system automatically refers officers with certain types and numbers of complaints accrued within a year;[113] the referral triggers a structured one-year training program with monthly monitoring reports to a committee and to the chief. The program can compel counseling or reassignment; if dissatisfied after a year, the reviewers can recommend termination.[114] Chief Watson described the program as "quite successful."[115]

The Long Beach Police Department established an officer-tracking system to hold officers and their supervisors accountable for problems in the community, ranging from conflict of any type to lawsuits, dog bites, and use-of-force complaints.[116] The department also has a system that requires an officer to detail any use of force to his or her sergeant. After separate investigations and reports by the sergeant and the supervising lieutenant, the case passes to the bureau chief, who reviews the incident. To enforce the reporting system, which was met with resistance, the department had to "audit and control" the system.[117] Since 1987, the Long Beach police have been monitoring radio transmissions between officers for racial slurs and misconduct.[118]

In the St. Louis County Police Department, the Bureau of Internal Affairs has the responsibility to "identify patterns and causes of citizen complaints and administer a counseling program to prevent similar complaints."[119] The Chief of the St. Louis Metropolitan Police Department testified that his department's system consists of a job-performance review process that analyzes data regarding police shootings, citizen complaints, and resisting-arrest cases. The officer and his or her commanding officer are brought in and counseled. If the reviewing officials think the officer has a problem, he or she receives training or counseling or is removed. The chief testified that he was not convinced the current system was adequate.[120]

The chief of operations for the Norfolk Police Department, Maj. Sheldon Darden, testified that he personally monitors all officers who use force in his bureau to find those who overuse it.[121] If his department, in the course of investigating an officer for misconduct, determines that another officer failed to report the misconduct, this second officer is also disciplined. Polygraphs are used in such situations.[122]

A number of police departments have established stress management programs as part of their mechanisms for detecting patterns of misconduct. In Chesapeake, Virginia, the police department provides supervisors with "stress profiles" to educate them on how to recognize signs of increasing stress. Supervisors can compel an officer to participate in the "employees assistance program" when he or she shows symptoms of stress.[123] Similarly, a representative of the Virginia Beach Police Department testified that it was in the process of training supervisors to recognize signs of stress. This department also has an employee assistance program to which officers are sent for counseling "after bad incidents."[124]

In the Miami Police Department, officers may be referred to outside "law-enforcement psychologists," who contract with the department to provide, among other things, employment services to officers experiencing psychological problems. The psychologists also offer stress management training. If officers experience particularly traumatic or stressful incidents, the psychologists provide "post-traumatic counseling" or "critical incident debriefing."[125]

Any Miami officer who discharges a weapon, whether or not it results in injury or death, must see the consulting psychologist before he or she can return to street patrol. According to one of the consulting psychologists, discharge of a firearm may indicate a problem that should be addressed in the police department.[126]

There are limitations in some departments on the power of the chief to take disciplinary action against officers. In Houston, state law allows termination decisions to be appealed to outside arbitrators, who reversed 60 percent of former Chief Brown's terminations.[127] Efforts by the city counsel and forty-one other cities to overturn the law were unsuccessful.[128] In Indianapolis, state law also limits the authority of the chief of police to discipline officers.[129] In Virginia Beach, police officers can appeal disciplinary actions to the city manager, then to a board of civilians authorized to review the chief's decisions, and then to court. The chief of the Virginia Beach Police Department testified that on two occasions in which he had recommended dismissal the board returned the officer to the street.[130]

D Civilians Seldom Prevail in Complaints Against Police Officers

1 Finding: Citizens are afraid to complain to the police about police misconduct

Citizens and representatives of community organizations at each of the hearings testified that many people are afraid to come forward to complain about police misconduct or to testify against officers.[131] There was testimony in several cities that African Americans complain within the black community, but often do not file formal complaints with their local police departments.[132]

Some citizens fear a complaint will result in retaliation by the police, ranging from harassment to criminal charges.[133] Witnesses to and victims of police misconduct fear they will be arrested if they complain about the police.[134] In Indianapolis, an African American clergyman described his fear of complaining to the police about misconduct:

> I'm scared to do it. I want to do it but I'm scared to do it because I have to live out there. . . . And I'm afraid, not so much for myself, but for my children. They go to school. . . . And I'm scared that, you know, the policeman may try to harass my children.[135]

Citizens also fear that the police will be unresponsive to complaints of misconduct.[136] When the president of the Houston Urban League advises victims of police misconduct to file complaints, she is often told it would be a waste of time; people generally believe "the police will be protected at all costs."[137] A St. Louis man described the attitude in his community toward filing complaints of police misconduct: "When you start to discuss . . . matters like this with individuals in my neighborhood, they feel like there is not going to be anything done about it, so why raise the issue."[138]

Citizens also feel that they are not listened to and that the police do not have an open mind about investigating citizen complaints.[139] There is a widespread belief that, even if the victim of abuse is not criminally charged, the police will question the victim's credibility simply because he or she is complaining against a police officer. The president of a local branch of the NAACP in Missouri described the community's lack of faith in police complaint processes bluntly: "[T]here is a complaint process. . . . But if I may use this scenario to describe it to you, it's like me being a black man complaining to the Grand Wizard that a Ku Klux Klan member hit me."[140] Even some police officials testified that, although they believe the community to be aware of the complaint process, citizens often have little confidence in it.[141]

Some victims of police abuse report incidents to community organizations, rather than pressing their own cases with the police departments, in the hope that these groups can do something on a wider basis.[142] For example, of twenty-one complaints provided to the Miami-Dade Branch of the NAACP during a twenty-month period (eleven of which involved excessive force), only two complainants were willing to come forward and provide sufficient evidence to allow the NAACP to pursue the complaint with the police department.[143]

Because of the fear of coming forward, the number of official complaints made to the police represents a small fraction of the number of citizens who have been the victims of police abuse. Even community and legal organizations that assist citizens with filing complaints or lawsuits alleging police misconduct hear about only a relatively small portion of the incidents of misconduct. As the president of the Urban League in Los Angeles testified:

> I don't think there is any doubt in anyone's mind for every complaint that was filed, there are many, many more out there. . . . Most people are discouraged, especially . . . where you have a predominance of African American residents. . . . [M]any more people out there . . . don't bother, because they know it is of no use.[144]

2 Finding: Procedures for civilian complaints of police misconduct are not widely publicized in the community

Those who are willing to file complaints about police behavior face a number of impediments. Primary among them is that many persons do not know what complaint systems are available to them, even though major urban police departments have formalized citizen complaint procedures.[145]

Several police representatives described the procedures in their departments for taking complaints from citizens. In most cities complaints can be made at any police station.[146] Some departments have rules that require the receiving officer to explain the complaint process and to assist the complainant in his or her filing.[147] Some police departments also have a written pamphlet explaining the citizen complaint process.[148]

Yet many citizens do not know where[149] or how to file a complaint[150] or what the complaint process is.[151] In areas with multiple law-enforcement agencies, people face the initial obstacle of properly identifying the police agency involved.[152] Smaller municipal police departments may not have formal, defined complaint procedures, but rather informal ones, such as coming in and talking to the police chief. Such an informal mechanism is often unknown to or intimidating to potential complainants.[153]

Some police officials testified that citizens may not be aware of the complaint process. For example, the new chief of the St. Louis Metropolitan Police Department testified, "Our problem is making [the complaint process] known and likely you are going to hear . . . complaints that people don't know about the process as to what it consist[s] of. . . ."[154]

3 Finding: Police discourage citizens from filing complaints of police misconduct

Many people reported that their attempts to file a complaint of misconduct are discouraged by the police departments.[155] They may actively resist the filing of the complaint by denying it then and there or by harassing the prospective complainant.[156]

The police discourage complaints by threatening to file or by filing criminal charges or civil lawsuits against victims of police misconduct. As described above, these victims (particularly the victims of the improper use of force) are frequently charged with criminal offenses ranging from disorderly conduct and destruction of property to assault on an officer and resisting arrest.[157]

Thus, they are not only brutalized but forced to confront the dangers—and cost—of being prosecuted. Fear of criminal punishment diverts victims' attention from pursuing complaints by making them use their limited resources for bail and counsel. A St. Louis man, who was stopped for speeding, was jailed, beaten, and charged with assault. He had to use his life savings to post bail and to hire a defense attorney. While he was hospitalized, his wife tried to file a complaint with the internal affairs division. She was discouraged by the police chief, who told her that he stood behind and believed his officer. The man who had been abused felt that there was no use in filing a complaint with the police.[158]

The use of criminal charges to deter complaints of police misconduct is not limited to the underlying incident. In Virginia Beach, an NAACP attorney was arrested and prosecuted for trespass when he went to the police station to file a complaint about police misconduct toward an NAACP observer at a major disturbance.[159] In Houston, a community activist was charged with making a false sworn statement in the course of an internal affairs complaint, creating a "chilling effect on . . . the citizens' willingness to make formal complaints regarding police misconduct."[160]

Prosecution of a citizen for statements made in the course of an investigation into police abuse sends a powerful message: the police will use the weight of the entire criminal justice system against citizens who complain about mistreatment. Prosecution of a prominent citizen, as in Virginia Beach, sends the message that there is an even greater risk of prosecution of less powerful members of the community.

On the other side of the coin is the silent acceptance of police perjury in this context. Far too frequently, prosecutors, judges, and attorneys encounter officers who lie under oath as part of their role in the adversary process.[161] Far too many officers lie with impunity about the conduct of a defendant, about what they were able to observe, and about whether proper procedures were followed. However, prosecutions of officers for perjury are extremely rare. It appears that since prosecutors must work with police officers they do not want to antagonize them.

The truth is that police officers are protected and civilians are not. Imposing a different and higher standard for citizens who complain of police misconduct fuels the perception that the word of a citizen—especially a minority citizen—is worthless.[162]

Some police officers use the *threat* of criminal charges to discourage the filing of a complaint. A St. Louis woman testified that she went to the police station to complain about being beaten outside her home; her brother had also been beaten and had been charged with resisting arrest (he was later acquitted). A sergeant told her that she should be arrested for "interference." She was told to read something posted on the wall, which described the penalties for making a false complaint. The woman testified she felt the police were trying to "put fear into her" to discourage her from filing the complaint.[163]

Similarly, citizens are sometimes threatened with civil lawsuits when they complain about police misconduct. Finding themselves in a position of considerable inequality in resources and power, they are often unwilling to run the risk of filing a complaint against the police. Joyce Armstrong of the St. Louis ACLU testified that people who went to the police to report abuse were reminded that they could be sued if they put anything "wrong" in their statements. As a result, the complainants wavered in their determination.[164]

In some police departments there is evidence of increasingly aggressive action against complainants. An Indianapolis lawyer testified that the police have been bringing SLAPP suits (strategic lawsuits against public participation). When many people in the community openly challenged three police shootings and the subsequent investigations, one of the citizens who questioned the police was "sued for essentially saying that he felt there was a cover-up."[165] The Boston Police Patrolmen's Association has announced it is planning to file libel lawsuits against citizens who have "made false allegations against officers."[166] The Christopher Commission found that some complainants were threatened by the LAPD with defamation suits or referrals to the Immigration and Naturalization Service.[167]

The police also discourage the filing of complaints in more subtle ways. They appear uninterested in a citizen's story, or they hide behind a stony, bureaucratic proceduralism.[168] Some complainants are advised (often contrary to regulations) that there are steps the department must complete before an officer may speak with them.[169] Others are told, "Don't call us, we'll call you"—a message too many citizens receive.[170] In some localities, the filing of a complaint precludes other governmental agencies from investigating it.[171]

A Los Angeles witness described an all-too-common scenario:

And then I filed a complaint. I went to the North Lewis Division, and I got information on how to file a complaint. And then he laughed, "Oh, the Airport Division. Yeah, I know them, and they are good guys up there." Well, I'm here to file a complaint. "Oh, a complaint," and they tried to give me the run around and I tried to file a complaint for maybe a week, and after that I left it alone and gave up on it.[172]

Complainants are also intimidated when police departments request that they sign an agreement not to discuss the case with anyone else, including the news media.[173] Most citizens do not believe they can refuse a police request, even if it seems to violate their First Amendment rights.

Officers also discourage eyewitnesses from complaining of police misconduct. Witnesses testified that the police treated them as if they were both incredible and blameworthy. For example, an African American man who called the police after seeing a young black man beaten by white officers in a St. Louis parking lot was asked more questions about himself than about the incident. "[W]e got into an argument because I tried to explain to him that I thought he should take a look at it and he just argued with me."[174] The witness was told that he could not file a complaint without the victim coming in, too. "[The police] discouraged me . . . until I just decided not to say anything else about it. . . . [They] made me feel like a nobody," he said.[175]

Civilian witnesses recounting police misconduct are treated with hostility and suspicion.[176] The police look for inconsistencies in their statements.[177] They sometimes investigate and intimidate witnesses.[178] If witnesses contradict some part of the complaint, it is often dismissed as "unfounded."

4 Finding: There is overwhelming citizen dissatisfaction with police investigations of citizen complaints

Citizens and representatives of community organizations in each city described deficiencies in the internal police complaint processes, ranging from the initiation stage to the results of the police investigations.[179] Many people rejected altogether the notion that police can police themselves.[180] When departments do not maintain adequate records of the prior misconduct of individual officers, civilian credibility suffers further.[181]

Civilians cannot hope to match the police resources that support officers in major investigations. A Miami witness testified that when there are shooting cases in the city a "shooting team" is assembled, which includes a prosecutor, homicide detectives, high-ranking police officials, internal review investigators, a public information officer, and the lawyer for the police benevolent association, among others. The officers are advised not to talk to anyone except the police attorney. "It appears that usually this team is working to clear the officer, not to make sure that justice is done," commented the witness.[182]

Investigations into police misconduct are quite different from ordinary police investigations into crime. The police often do not even look for witnesses in misconduct cases. Nor do they come into the community to try to do a full and fair investigation.[183] If witnesses are known, they are often interviewed on police territory. When witnesses are interviewed, their information may not be recorded if it is damaging to the officer.[184] Little or no weight may be given to physical evidence suggesting abuse.[185]

Many cases of police misconduct take place out of the public eye. Often, there are no witnesses to the incident other than police officers and the victim of the misconduct, and thus no one to corroborate the complainant's account.[186] Representatives of community organizations and legal agencies described the difficulty of pursuing complaints against the police, particularly in the absence of witnesses.[187] Both police and civilians agreed that, if it comes down to a citizen's word against an officer's story, the police version controls. In the vast majority of cases involving one civilian and one officer the complaint is not sustained.[188] The outcome is the same when there is a lack of "independent corroboration."[189]

Departments often categorize the disposition of complaints of police misconduct into "sustained," "not sustained," "unfounded," and "exonerated." "Not sustained" is generally defined as a conclusion that there is insufficient evidence to prove or disprove the allegation of misconduct. The designations "not sustained" and "unfounded" contribute to the general perception that citizens are not believed; the language suggests a rejection of the claim, not that a level of proof was not met. The most frequent disposition of citizen complaints is "not sustained."[190]

Some police officials in the hearings acknowledged the demoralizing effect on citizens that results from the practice of not sustaining complaints. For example, a representative of the Board of Governors for Law Enforcement Officials of Greater St. Louis testified:

> The problem is that in many of these cases it is impossible to make the decision one way or the other because there is no other evidence. The officer denies it. I was doing my job. They come up with some justification. The citizen therefore gets a letter back from the police department saying we have investigated your complaint, and it is non-sustained. We cannot prove or disprove what took place. And certainly a citizen in that situation is going to feel that something happened to them that was not right. The police department does not care and doesn't do anything about it.[191]

Certain police practices undermine the complaint process before an allegation is even investigated. First, the practice of criminally charging a potential complainant—not a criminal defendant—allows the police to not take him or her seriously.[192] The police simply cast the complaint of misconduct as retaliatory.[193]

The complainant alleging police misconduct knows that he or she is seen first and foremost as a *defendant*. A witness at the Norfolk hearings testified, "[Y]ou have a lot of pending charges that are intimidating and you're coming to Internal Affairs and after you give this written statement and recorded statement they will inform [you] that your statements have nothing to do with helping your case."[194]

Second, even if the complainant is not criminally charged in connection with the incident, police often use a prior criminal record as evidence of the complainant's lack of credibility. A Norfolk witness testified:

> [B]ut it always comes down to, especially in the case of the African American citizen, no matter who you are, when something happens involving you, it comes down to a credibility thing, whether anybody can believe you, and when you have a person that has a clean record, a nice background, then their case will receive better support than would a case of a man who may have been in trouble a year ago, but he may have not been doing anything that particular night.[195]

Third, while thorough, aggressive investigations serve a legitimate truth-seeking function, questioning witnesses in a disrespectful and derisive manner undermines the integrity of an investigation. Not only does a hostile investigation discourage witnesses from coming forward with evidence, it also improperly shapes the testimony given. Under such conditions, answers are bound to be monosyllabic and nondescriptive.

The Christopher Commission found that labeling a witness "independent" or "involved" often determined whether the complaint was sustained by the LAPD. More than 50 percent of the unsustained cases alleging excessive force lacked independent witnesses.[196]

While the relationship between complainant and witness may be relevant in assessing accounts of misconduct, police too often use minimal connections to discredit witness accounts. For example, in one case reviewed by the Christopher Commission, a witness was designated by investigators as being "involved" simply because he had reported the incident.[197]

Many police officials testified that their departments have specific policies for completing investigations of citizen complaints within a specified time frame and for notifying complainants of the outcome of investigations.[198] However, citizens complained that they are not kept informed of the status of the investigations and that there are long delays in their completion.[199] Complainants are frequently frustrated by delay and silence,[200] and by their complaints "going nowhere."[201]

For example, Judy Steen Davis filed a complaint regarding the Metro-Dade Police beating of her husband, her thirteen-year-old daughter, and herself in 1988. Though she was told the investigation would be done in sixty days, it was not completed until eighteen months after she was acquitted of assaulting the officer and resisting arrest. The officers were exonerated.[202]

Some police officials testified that they had recently revised their departments' policies regarding the investigation of civilian complaints. For example, the chief of the Chesapeake Police Department testified that, after the Rodney King incident, he and his staff reviewed their internal affairs policies, complaints, and statistics. They also reviewed charges of assault on police officers to determine whether those who made the charges were the same officers who received internal affairs complaints.[203]

As a result of this review, and the discovery that most of the complaints involved one-on-one confrontations without witnesses, the department revised its internal affairs policies. The new procedure requires three bureau commanders to review an internal investigation for completeness, including determining whether a real effort was made to find witnesses. The bureau commanders make a joint recommendation. All investigations must be completed within thirty days unless the chief gives an extension because of unavailable witnesses or pending criminal or civil litigation.[204]

The Long Beach Police Department also undertook an investigation of its complaint procedures after receiving criticism from the community. The chief of police testified:

> There is a gentleman in the audience today . . . who complained to me that our organization did not take police complaints from members of the community. I initially disagreed with him, but after we did some audits and stings, we found his allegations were true. The organization was very reluctant to take personnel complaints which caused a demotion of some of our supervisors.[205]

The chief of police in Signal Hill, California, testified that his department had also changed its internal affairs process.

Specifically, he testified that internal affairs was placed under his supervision. He now personally directs any investigation and holds daily briefings. Additionally, the department developed a new form to assist citizens in filing a complaint of misconduct and distributed it at city hall as well as at the police department.[206] According to Chief McCrary, citizens have been invited to meet with him to discuss investigations, and "just about in every case they felt they were treated fairly and allowed [him] to improve the trust level."[207]

5 Finding: Citizens rarely prevail in police investigations

The consensus of the citizens and representatives of community organizations who testified at the hearings is that the internal review investigators overwhelmingly side with the police, generally concluding that the officer(s) used proper force.[208] Many felt the internal affairs complaint process was a waste of time.[209]

Even police witnesses acknowledged that police investigators, out of the desire to protect other officers from sanctions, have a tendency to discourage complaints or to skew outcomes in favor of the police.[210] In addition, an officer's desire to protect his own career in the department may serve as an incentive to find for the police rather than for the citizen.[211] Another reason for the bias of the outcomes of the investigations may be the desire to protect a self-insured city against liability.[212]

The information given by some police agencies provides support for the citizens' perception of the outcomes of investigations. The chief of the Virginia Beach Police Department testified that approximately 13 percent of the 127 complaints of excessive or inappropriate force had been sustained by the department.[213] From 1986 to 1990, 65 complaints of excessive force were investigated by the internal affairs division of the St. Louis County Police Department, but the allegations were sustained and the officers disciplined in only 4 cases (6 percent).[214] In 1990, citizens filed 13 complaints alleging excessive use of force by St. Louis County police officers, with the following dispositions: one complaint was withdrawn by the complaining witness; one case was closed because the complaining witness "wouldn't cooperate"; two were investigated by the FBI; three cases were pending as of December 1991; three were not resolved because the investigation was inconclusive; officers in two cases were exonerated; and one officer resigned before the investigation of his case was completed.[215]

Whether a complaint is sustained by police investigators often depends on the nature of the allegation or the identity of the complainant. The director of the Metro-Dade Police Department testified that one-third of the complaints were sustained in his department and that the department took disciplinary action (firing, counseling, or new training) depending upon the nature of the complaint.[216] However, only twenty-one complaints of "unauthorized force" were sustained by the Metro-Dade Police Department in the years 1985–90.[217] The number of sustained complaints represented only 6 percent of the total complaints of unauthorized force during that period.[218]

In its review of the LAPD police investigations of more than thirty-four hundred citizen complaints of excessive force or improper tactics from 1986 through 1990, the Christopher Commission found that only 3 percent of the allegations were sustained, while 47 percent were "not sustained" and 37.8 percent were classified as "unfounded."[219] Similarly, the St. Clair

Commission found the overall rate of sustained complaints in the Boston Police Department to be 5.9 percent.[220] The percentage of cases alleging physical abuse that were sustained by Boston's internal affairs department dropped from 11 percent in 1989 to 3 percent in 1990.[221]

A complaint that arises within the police department is more likely to be sustained than one made by a citizen. For example, a disproportionate percentage of the small number of complaints sustained by the Boston Police Department were "allegations brought by the [d]epartment itself for violation of [d]epartmental rules."[222] Similarly in Los Angeles, a *Daily News* investigation revealed that 5 percent of 1,488 complaints filed against the LAPD arose within the department; 53.7 percent of these were sustained. By contrast, citizens made 95 percent of the complaints, but these were sustained by the LAPD in only 4.6 percent of the cases.[223] Witnesses in Los Angeles testified that violations of departmental regulations are far more likely to be disciplined than are allegations of brutality.[224] Of 106 officers in the LAPD who were found guilty of brutality, 13 percent were terminated, while 44 percent were suspended for five days or less.[225] As the St. Clair report noted,

> the extremely low percentage of sustained cases in the Boston area indicates that, in the view of the Boston Police Department, 94% of the citizens alleging misconduct were incorrect. This statistic strains the imagination; it assumes that more than 9 out of every ten citizens who complain of police misconduct are either mistaken or lying.[226]

6 Finding: Civil lawsuits rarely provide relief to victims of police abuse

Civil suits for personal injuries or false arrest are generally not a viable avenue of redress for victims of police misconduct.

Few lawyers will take such cases. There are considerable financial disincentives to litigating cases of police abuse.[227] Most victims cannot afford to pay an attorney in advance.[228] Moreover, because attorneys generally accept these cases on a contingency-fee basis, most will not pursue them unless they conclude that the complainant is likely to prevail on the facts and that the damage award will be so substantial that it would justify the commitment of time and resources required in such litigation.[229]

Cases of misconduct involving verbal abuse or humiliation, short-term detention after a false arrest, or minor injuries are not likely to be litigated at all. The most common complaints, and the most common forms of police overstepping—officers handcuffing arrested persons too tightly, shoving them into squad cars and police wagons too roughly, being generally abusive and derisive—are unlikely to get beyond a confidential communication to criminal defense counsel. As a result, the definition of police brutality is pushed higher and higher. Rodney King gets attention. Alexander Kelly does not.[230] Being roughed up by the police is seen as an acceptable part of the arrest process.

The length of time between filing suit and its resolution discourages some attorneys from taking cases of police misconduct.[231] The cost of bringing such suits is prohibitive, even if the victim finds an attorney who will litigate on a contingency-fee basis. Litigants must come up with money for filing fees, medical examinations, travel expenses, expert witness fees, psychiatric evaluations, and depositions.[232] In addition, in some jurisdictions there is a legal limit on the amount that victims of police misconduct can recover in such suits.[233] Most police officers do not have to pay the costs of litigation personally. Typically, a police union or the city itself provides legal representation and covers the litigation costs. The average citizen cannot match the resources of the police officers defending such suits.[234]

In addition, only a limited number of attorneys are willing to take on the police. Some may fear the consequences of alienating a department they will have to deal with in the future. Others may be more inclined to believe the police version than the account of a citizen, particularly one with a criminal record or one who faces criminal charges in connection with the encounter with the police.

Even those attorneys who are familiar with the reality of police misconduct and are sympathetic to victims recognize the difficulty of prevailing in court. An African American attorney in Indianapolis testified:

> [T]here is a general cynicism on the part of any citizen that feels they have a complaint, as well as any attorney who is in a position to have to defend a client where there have been these multiple allegations of misdemeanor counts. And also with respect to being able to take a case of police harassment or brutality successfully to any kind of civil conclusion.[235]

Since most victims of police abuse have neither documentation of the incident nor independent witnesses, the jury must decide whether the victim of the abuse or the police officer(s) is more credible. The verdict in the first Rodney King case is but one example that, given a choice, jurors will generally decide in favor of the police. The verdict in the second Rodney King case shows that in the face of enhanced, irrefutable documentation of abuse and public pressure to hold *someone* responsible, jurors may sometimes convict police officers. Note that the second jury also acquitted police officers.[236] A St. Louis ACLU attorney testified that her office has taken the position that in most cases where it is the word of the individual citizen against the word of police officers, litigation is not a "reasonable choice"; instead, her office collects the information to monitor for patterns of misconduct.[237]

E There Seems to Be a Correlation Between the Race of the Officer, the Race of the Citizen, and the Incidence of Abuse

1 Finding: Minority citizens report greater violence at the hands of white officers

Witnesses report that white police violence against black citizens is more likely to occur than is black police violence against white citizens. Many people in the minority community believe that white police officers are far more responsible for abusive conduct toward minorities than any other group. George E. Mins, president of the Virginia Beach NAACP, believes that "statistically it's more often a white officer and a black citizen, but there are some cases of black officers being involved in force cases as well."[238] Rev. Jew Don Boney testified in Houston that there are "indeed some black officers who are guilty of misconduct," but that he was unable to find any example of a black officer accidentally shooting anyone. In contrast, "over and over, again and again, white officers accidentally shoot and kill citizens, and somehow are found innocent of any wrongdoing."[239]

Rickie Clark, of the National Black Police Association, testified that his organization has yet to receive a complaint from a white person claiming mistreatment by a black officer. They have had no reports from the community regarding a black officer shooting a white suspect. African American officers have been involved in shootings, but not under circumstances that led to a major response from the community.[240]

The authors of this book concede that there is little hard data to support the extensive anecdotal evidence that the worst incidents of police abuse, and the majority of cases of police abuse, are committed by white officers on nonwhite citizens. Nonetheless, we stand by the assertion. Police abuse in America largely consists of white officers abusing minority citizens.

Norfolk Attorney Bernard T. Holmes agreed that it is hard to make a conclusive statement about how officers treat minority citizens. He testified that there is a need to develop a database to get a concrete picture of the treatment of minorities by officers.[241]

State senator Diane Watson of California testified that a lack of hard data allows a police department to deny discriminatory conduct.[242] Therefore, departments should be "required to categorize incidents of police abuse based upon the race, religion, ethnicity, age, citizenship status, politics, economic condition, sex, and sexual orientation of victims and to publish that information periodically."[243]

Carol Heppe, of Police Watch, asserted that "[k]nowledge about the problem of [police misconduct] on a national scale is essential."[244] She testified that the federal government has a duty to compile statistics on state prosecutions of the police and to conduct studies of police abuse in its capacity as guarantor of the civil and human rights of all U.S. citizens.[245] It has, she said, "failed to collect and keep essential data about violations and has maintained unnecessary restrictions on the power of the federal government to protect human rights against police abuse."[246]

There are also few statistics on the degree to which minority officers involve themselves in police misconduct. There is a popular perception that black police officers are less involved in misconduct than are their white colleagues. James Beauford, of the Urban League in St. Louis, reported that there had been a "low number" of African American officers involved in police shootings.[247]

Nonetheless, Mr. Beauford testified, a study commissioned by the St. Louis Metropolitan Police Department found that its officers used their weapons "much too much"; furthermore, it was "not just a black/white issue, it was black officers using their weapons too much as well."[248]

2 Finding: African American police officers may be under pressure to tolerate racially motivated police abuse to keep their jobs

African American police officers may face more pressure than their white counterparts to keep silent about police abuse to ensure continued employment and promotion opportunities. There was testimony in the hearings about black officers needing to make a good impression on white officers or superiors in order to get ahead.

Witnesses testified that African American officers are not immune to the pull of the code of silence. Col. William H. Young of the St. Louis Black Leadership Round Table observed:

"[T]hat mind set exist[s] and it really crosses all racial barriers too. . . . It is considered to be a part of the brotherhood to be a part of the police department."[249] Other witnesses testified that African American officers fear losing their jobs and will not report misconduct because there is no support system if they do so. If one officer reports misconduct by another, the "question then becomes whose side are you on?"[250]

Black police officers are in a much different position from their white colleagues. In most departments, white officers dominate leadership positions, controlling the decision-making processes and setting the standards for behavior. African American officers are in a double bind. Knowing they may not have the same access to the upper command staff, black officers may find it to their benefit to keep quiet about the racially motivated abuse they see and even to participate in it. However, the code of silence in a department may protect whites more than blacks. White officers who may not be willing to inform on colleagues of their own race may not feel the same way about black police officers.[251]

There are risks to speaking out against fellow members of the force for minority officers. After watching police beat a young black suspect in 1970 in Alexandria, Virginia, Herman E. Springs complained to his supervisor about the abusive conduct and refused to go back out onto the street with those involved. Though the officer responsible for the beating was fired, there were reprisals for Herman Springs. He was sent out on calls by a dispatcher into a different patrol area, one he was not as familiar with. He was dispatched to violent domestic incidents without backup. He was sent on calls involving guns, and officers in the area refused to assist him.[252]

F There Is an "Us versus Them" Mentality in Police-Community Relations

1 Finding: A "code of silence" continues to exist in many police departments

The notion that there is a "code of silence," which protects and insulates police officers from allegations of misconduct, has been asserted for some time. It is a shared, often unspoken vow taken by police officers never to "rat" on each other. The most widely known example of the code of silence was described in the book (and then the movie, starring Al Pacino) *Serpico*,[253] which propelled the code into the popular culture. The lesson of *Serpico* was that, while police will back each other up on the most dangerous streets, no one will back a whistle-blower.

Many police officers deny that a code of silence exists.[254] Certainly, if they confirmed the existence of such a code they would be admitting something deeply disturbing about how police departments operate. The most obvious question raised would be why, unless there is substantial unethical or illegal activity taking place, the code needs to exist. Some officers say that the public does not fully recognize how dependent police officers are on their fellows. Conflict and dissension can put lives in danger. Police officers may rightly feel that they have only each other, that no one but another officer can know what it means to be a cop. Though military analogies are most often suggested, the tight camaraderie of police officers might also be likened to that of sports teams. None of these assertions convincingly argues against the existence of the code.

Citizens and representatives of community organizations in each city testified about the persistence of a police code of silence.[255] A St. Louis witness testified that it is a fact in many police departments. "Code of silence exists. It's the peer pressure of being accepted in the Department to be able to depend on each other to support each other."[256]

Part of the difficulty with criminal prosecutions of police officers lies in convincing a jury that it is in the public interest to convict bad members of a force. Juries, at least in most places, identify more with police officers than with the person assaulted or killed by the police, especially if that person has a criminal record. Jurors ask themselves whether they should sacrifice the police officer, who is just trying to protect them, or whether they should be a little generous under the circumstances.

Still, the central difficulty in obtaining criminal convictions of so-called bad cops is the unwillingness of other officers to come forward to testify to their misconduct. The power of testimony by police officers who witnessed police misconduct and are willing to testify cannot be overestimated.

Internal disciplining of bad officers may be even more difficult to obtain. Whether operating under a code of silence or not, police officers have always been loath to report on their colleagues, even internally and informally. At the very least, such reporting is disloyal. For those officers who feel they *must* come forward, there is no guarantee that the offender will be removed from the job. Thus, the complaining officer may find himself or herself out on a limb, possibly even working with the officer complained against.

What is interesting is that most members of a force know the identities of the bad cops. "Inside the department, we know who the problem officers are, it's just that nobody does anything about them," said a ranking Boston police officer, who asked that his name not be used.[257] Whether out of fear of retribution or something else, he was not willing to complain formally about the bad members of the force, but he was willing to provide anonymous information to the press.

Most police officers maintain, however, that there are only a few bad members of the force who give whole departments a bad name. The vast majority of their colleagues, they say, are hard-working cops who are disgusted with those officers who do the job poorly, harassing and intimidating the public in the process. Officers frequently complain that the bad cops draw all the attention, not the good ones, who honorably perform the job day in and day out.

What is obvious is that if we can identify those officers responsible for most of the misconduct, we should be able to discipline them or remove them from the force. This cannot be done without the voices of those officers who care about the quality—or at least the reputation—of the police. Whether silent officers are good cops or bad, their silence makes them accomplices of those who are bringing police departments down.

2 Finding: Police and elected officials vary widely in the opinions they voice regarding the prevalence of police misconduct and the code of silence

Many police officials acknowledged that departments have traditionally made frequent arrests in the black community and in low-income areas, with the result that many African Americans grow up under constant surveillance.[258] Often, the officials did not make a connection between racism and policing. The chief of the Virginia Beach Police Department testified that the perception that African Americans are more frequently police targets arises in part from a "lack of understanding and apprehension of police," which causes "initial strain." He attributed the police response to the stress involved in dealing with street drugs and voiced the opinion that a majority of drug dealers are black.[259] Some police officials complained that the media create and reinforce perceptions that African Americans are targets of excessive force.[260]

Some elected officials testified that, although incidents of police brutality still occurred, they have been far less frequent in recent years.[261] Some testified that their police department does not condone police misconduct and that it has aggressively tried to improve police-community relations.[262] Several police officials testified that it was the policy of their department not to tolerate brutality and that it was important for the department to strictly enforce that policy.[263]

While many citizens testified that police misconduct is an ongoing and pervasive problem and that police-community relations in their communities are at a low point, some citizens testified that there has been overall improvement in police-community relations and in the frequency of police misconduct.[264] Several of the same citizens, however, testified that there are still officers who display a pattern of misconduct, yet remain on the force.[265]

African American officers in a number of the cities took a leading role in acknowledging the reality of police brutality. Rickie Clark, a member of the National Black Police Association (NBPA), testified that police brutality is a "routine fact of police life."[266] The chairman of the Ethical Society of Police in St. Louis testified that the Rodney King tape had done little to "deter or prevent incidents of brutality" in his area.[267] Shelby

Lanier, a member of the NBPA in Louisville, Kentucky, testified that his organization had been founded to help eliminate police brutality.[268] Herman E. Springs, a member of the National Organization of Black Law Enforcement Executives (NOBLE),[269] testified at the Norfolk hearings that the group "has complained for years that residents are disrespected, disregarded, physically and verbally abused."[270] The vice-president of the Miami Chapter of NOBLE testified that "police brutality and . . . beating confessions out of suspects are not so common now, as they were . . . in the late 1920's and early 1930's. What does remain is institutionalized malpractice and various procedures which violate the laws or the constitutional rights or the human dignity of civilians."[271] In the view of NOBLE, community-police relations are at an all-time low.[272] Members of the organization also described the practice of making arrests in order to try to legally justify the use of force.[273]

African American law-enforcement groups also took a leading role in proposing concrete steps to confront police brutality. According to members who testified at the hearings, NBPA and NOBLE are committed to speaking up and taking action against police misconduct.[274] The chairman of the Ethical Society of Police in St. Louis, a charter member of the National Black Police Association, testified:

> If any officer commits an act of police brutality in the presence of any member of the Ethical Society of Police, our member will attempt to stop the illegal act, arrest the officer if the officer refuse[s] to stop and call for assistance in effecting the arrest if necessary. We will initiate criminal charges against the violators. . . .[275]

Members of NOBLE emphasized the need to let the community know that African American officers will not tolerate abuse of citizens by the police and testified that NOBLE has pledged both to raise the national consciousness about police brutality and to work with community groups to combat police abuse.[276] Similarly, NBPA pledges to stand by to assist the victims of police abuse and recognizes the need to enlist the support of the community to stop it.[277]

In contrast to civilian witnesses, some police officials denied that any code of silence existed.[278] Other police officials asserted that although the code existed,[279] it was not as prevalent as in years past,[280] and that it would not be condoned by their police department.[281]

The director of the Metro-Dade Police Department testified that officers are coming forward against other officers with increasing frequency.[282] Houston prosecutor Don Smyth testified that newer officers are more willing "to come forward and tell us about their fellow officers who are not doing what they should," but are more reluctant to "get up there and testify against them."[283]

In contrast, several African American officers who testified explicitly acknowledged the prevalence of the code of silence,[284] and, in some instances, perjury by fellow officers.[285] One witness testified that in his twenty-one years in law enforcement a code of silence has always been a practice.[286]

Testimony from current or former police officers in a number of different cities reveals a dangerous lack of support for those who complain about the misconduct of fellow officers. Witnesses testified that there can be repercussions within the department as a result of such complaints,[287] ranging from being confronted with "trumped up charges"[288] to not getting backup in answering calls while on patrol.[289]

A former Metro-Dade officer in field training in 1990 was told by her officers that "snitches were not tolerated and members of the profession fight for themselves. . . . An officer . . . told me, 'We take care of our own.' "[290] Upon refusing to obey a superior officer's command to "take down" an African American suspect with force, she was offered the "choice" of demotion or termination. "It is no coincidence that anyone speaking the truth . . . is subject to severe consequences."[291] A member of the African-American Police Officers League in Houston said that there is a "code of silence . . . any time you speak out or identify anything, you're singled out . . . [and] retaliated against."[292]

The Christopher Commission also found that officers in the LAPD who gave testimony against other members of the force were frequently harassed and ostracized and sometimes became the target of internal complaints.[293] Recognizing the likelihood of retaliation against officers who report abuse by their colleagues, NOBLE has pledged to support the reporting officers.[294]

Some police officials testified that officers who did not cooperate with internal affairs investigations into allegations of non-criminal misconduct could be and were dismissed.[295] Others testified that if an officer is found guilty of misconduct and the department discovers that another officer has not reported it this second officer is also subject to discipline.[296]

3   Finding: Some police departments are attempting to move away from an "us versus them" attitude to a philosophy of cooperation with the community

Many of the police departments described the need to move away from the traditional "us versus them" mentality and the rapid-response and crime-solving approaches to policing.[297] Some conceded the failure of such an approach in combating crime. As Chief Watson of Houston said: "[W]e are victims of our own success. We have done a very good job of arresting a lot of people. Our prisons are filled to overflowing. And yet we continue to be pressed with demands for service that are ever increasing, and continue to need additional officers."[298]

Police officials at the hearings—even those from rural departments—generally endorsed the concept of community policing, described by Chief Watson as "neighborhood-oriented policing" and "working cooperatively with our citizens."[299] Chief Harmon of the St. Louis Metropolitan Police Department testified that community policing is "the cornerstone of my administration."[300] Maj. Dennis R. Long of the St. Louis County Police Department testified that his department was "just beginning to get into the area of community policing."[301] The superintendent of the Missouri State Highway Patrol testified that the principles of community policing are beginning to be followed in the smaller cities of Missouri.[302]

Community policing means a change in attitude toward the community. Director Taylor of the Metro-Dade Police Department said his department's philosophy "is to deal with a more human, more proper way with the citizens of this community and where they live and what they want."[303]

Community policing recognizes the complexities of multicultural urban communities. As Chief Calvin Ross of Miami testified:

Policing in the nineties can no longer survive with the "we versus they" attitude. . . . Policing in the nineties demands change. . . . Each police department across this nation must take into account the cultural dynamics of its constit[uents] and consider themselves as servants, first. . . . [T]here must be an understanding of the role of the police in the community as being part of the community. . . . [E]ach police agency [must] become thoroughly familiar with and understand the culture, the problems and needs of the entire community and devise programs to be responsive. . . . [T]he personnel makeup . . . [must] be a reflection of the community it serves. . . .[304]

Chief Harmon of the St. Louis Metropolitan Police Department testified his department is beginning to teach against the "us versus them" mentality as part of its COPS (Community Oriented Policing Services) program and of cultural diversity training.[305]

Police witnesses said community policing also means a change in methodology. Houston's Chief Watson spoke of the need for "expand[ing] the role of officers . . . look[ing] at the underlying caus[es] of a situation and at what happens after the arrest occurs."[306] Chief Ross of Miami testified:

Whether [allegations of police abuse] are real or perceived the allegations are symptomatic of a deep rooted problem in the methodology in Florida by police. . . . Policing in the nineties must focus more on the prevention of crime than the band aide [sic] solution of reactive measures.[307]

A witness in St. Louis described the reciprocal nature of this approach: "Community policing is not a one way process, it requires that residents get actively involved, that they work closely with [their] assigned police officers to locate problems from nagging nuisance to serious crimes and then determine, together, ways to solve them."[308] Chief Harmon of the St. Louis

Metropolitan Police Department testified, "The police can't . . . function and ought not to in a democracy without strong and continual citizen involvement of input."[309]

Many police officials emphasized the need for better communication between the police and the community.[310] For some, such communication (and communication inside the force) bears directly on the effectiveness of the department. Chief Shipley of the Chesapeake Police Department testified, "Communication is the key to understanding and understanding is the key to corrective actions."[311]

Many police officials testified there are real benefits to a community policing approach. For example, Superintendent Fisher of the Missouri State Highway Patrol testified that there is "no question that community involvement and joint problem solving is beneficial."[312] Major Long of the St. Louis County Police Department, describing the impact of his department's community service programs on the "us versus them" mentality, testified: "I think it's something that we probably were guilty of at one time, but I feel that we've come a long way and are hopefully on the right track now."[313] The mayor of Chesapeake testified that protests from the black community in 1986 had led to a series of meetings, improved communication, and better police-community relations.[314]

An African American officer in St. Louis testified that community-oriented policing would be a "big help in reconnecting an officer to the community" and would break down the code of silence because the officers "will feel like they are a part of the community. It won't be us against them. It would be us period."[315]

An official in the St. Louis County Police Department described the promise of community policing:

I think it's going to be the thing of the future and I would hope that we can expand that and I would like the day to come when a survey would be taken of our citizens and that the majority of them, not just the majority, a high percentage, hopefully unanimous, would voice confidence in our ability to deliver service that would be tailored to [their] needs and they feel that we really do care about them.[316]

4 Finding: There must be greater inclusion of minorities in police departments and police decision making

Shelby Lanier of the National Black Police Association believes that African American police officers and citizens should take the lead in addressing the problem of racism and police brutality against minorities. He testified that "[i]t is our position that the solutions [to] the problem of police brutality [are] now in the hands of the African American police officers and African American citizens."[317]

Many of those who testified at the hearings believed that much of the "us versus them" problem grows out of an underrepresentation of minorities on the police force and in decision-making roles in law enforcement. Recent events in Los Angeles, New York, Detroit, Nashville, and Minneapolis seem to support this view.[318] Professor Marvin Jones, of the University of Miami School of Law, believes that the underrepresentation of blacks in the executive branch, the legislative branch, and the judicial branch of all governments, and in local law enforcement, contributes to the problem.[319]

State senator Diane Watson of California testified that unchecked abuse of power by a largely white police force and the lack of effective leadership in the highest ranks of the department contribute to the spread of racism:

> Prejudice plus power equals racism, and it will be hard to prove that prejudice has played no part in the selective abuse to which residents of Los Angeles have been and continue to be subjected. Much of the problems in the LAPD can be attributed to a tone of indifference that starts from the top. . . .[320]

Witnesses in several cities expressed similar views. For example, there was testimony in Miami, Houston, Norfolk, and St. Louis that there are not enough African Americans in upper-level positions in police departments. As one witness in Miami testified, in describing the Metro-Dade Police Department, African Americans and other minorities are disenfranchised in the department, and there is a serious need for more minorities in decision-making positions above the rank of lieutenant.[321]

Others went further by recommending that more black and Latino officers be assigned to specific jurisdictions, making assignments to certain neighborhoods by race if necessary. According to these witnesses, for example, there should be more African American officers assigned to patrol black communities and more Puerto Rican officers assigned to patrol Puerto Rican communities.[322]

Dr. Larry Capp testified that police-science research shows there is better policing if officers know an area, live there, and have families there—they know the community and the community knows them. When police reflect the community, there is less use of force and fewer brutality complaints. Trust and confidence are enhanced, and suspicion and apprehension dissipate.[323]

Perhaps there ought to be a system of rewards for police

officers who make community ties. Testimony from the Miami-Dade Branch of the NAACP included a recommendation that officers who involve themselves in community activities receive credit for "pro-social behavior."[324]

Of course, more must be done than simply hiring more minority police officers. As discussed above, police brutality is cultural as well as racial. There is a need for standards and a need for constant oversight of the conduct of police, white and black. Sam Jones, of the Urban League of Indianapolis, testified that the community must take more responsibility for keeping the issue of police misconduct in minority communities alive at all times, not just in times of crisis.[325]

> [W]e African Americans have to demand of our Police Department fair and equitable law enforcement in our community. We in this community tend to be reactive as oppose[d] to . . . proactive in terms of law enforcement. We act when a shooting occurs. We react on reported brutality. . . . [W]e need to be proactive.[326]

The minority community must have a clearer vision of the goals it sets for itself and the means it selects to achieve them. It will not be enough to state simply that more minorities should be hired. While this may be one valid goal, it fails to address some of the problems the minority community has with minority police officers, as well as with crime, generally.

5 Finding: There has been an increase in minority representation in many police departments, but some departments continue to fail to reflect the communities they serve

A number of police and city officials testified at the hearings that the police must recognize the cultural diversity in their cities and increase the representation of minorities and women in police departments.[327] Mayor Hudnut of Indianapolis testified that the police department must recruit, hire, and promote officers on the basis of the demographics of the community, and that community persons must be given jobs in the police department that will include responsibilities in their neighborhoods.[328] Chief Elizabeth Watson of Houston testified that her department needed to "work aggressively toward making [the] police department representative at all ranks of the community that [it] serve[s]."[329]

Several officials testified that the aim of their departments was to have the percentages of minorities on the force equal the percentages of minorities in the population served by the department.[330] For example, Major Long of the St. Louis County Police Department stated, "[O]ur goal of course would be to have a number of minorities equal to the population of the area we serve . . . that would hopefully be our minimum."[331]

Some of the departments have recruitment plans described by witnesses as "affirmative action" plans, ranging from written plans[332] to unwritten policies.[333] Others have no affirmative action plan of any kind.[334] The superintendent of the Missouri State Highway Patrol testified that recruiting minorities is a major part of its community relations program and that his department was committed to hiring "qualified minorities."[335] In Houston, witnesses testified that an affirmative action program for civilian appointments in the police department allows for greater flexibility in hiring minorities, but that it is against state law to have an affirmative action program as part of the hiring process in the police or fire department.[336] In some cities, affirmative action plans have been the result of lawsuits. For example, the United States Justice Department brought suit against the City of Miami, resulting in a 1984 consent decree.[337]

Several police departments have specifically targeted local organizations for minority recruitment. A number of departments—the St. Louis County Police Department and those in Norfolk, Virginia Beach, and Chesapeake, Virginia—direct recruiting efforts at black colleges, universities, and churches.[338] The Virginia Beach Police Department has contacted the local NAACP and sends recruiters to speak with officers who have been laid off from other forces.[339] Witnesses in Norfolk testified that representatives from the Norfolk and Chesapeake Police Departments attend job fairs to recruit potential officers.[340]

A number of police departments attempt to recruit from the military. The Houston Police Department targets military bases and persons with honorable discharges.[341] Representatives of the departments in Los Angeles and Norfolk testified that they also recruit from the military.[342]

Some police departments make use of the media in their recruiting efforts. The Los Angeles Police Department advertises in the press and on radio programs directed at minorities and uses the media to make public service announcements.[343] The Chesapeake Police Department has advertised in African American newspapers, and its representatives have spoken on minority radio stations.[344] Houston uses mass media and an advertising agency to recruit nationwide.[345]

Representatives of several police departments testified that they have developed new programs to increase minority representation. The chief of the St. Louis Metropolitan Police Department testified that his department has worked with the Urban League and a local business to sponsor a scholarship program at the University of Missouri, St. Louis: participants are given a four-year scholarship in the form of a loan to pursue a degree in criminal justice and can repay the loan by working in the police department for five years.[346] The Los Angeles Police Department provides materials to officers to do "one-on-one recruiting" among friends, relatives, and acquaintances. The LAPD also has pretraining of candidates to help ensure their success at the police academy.[347] In addition to other recruiting efforts, the Norfolk Police Department has held study sessions with the local Urban League to help teach police officers how to take a test.[348]

Officials of other police departments testified to proposals for changes in recruiting. The superintendent of the Missouri State Highway Patrol testified that his agency planned to become more active in high schools and hoped to establish soon an annual recruiting plan to provide goals and annual training for recruiters.[349] Miami's Chief Ross testified that his department was currently recruiting within the Haitian community to increase Haitian representation in the Miami Police Department.[350]

Some of the departments have significantly increased the number of minority officers on the force in recent years.[351] For example, in Miami minority representation increased from 42 percent of sworn officers in 1980 to 66 percent in 1990.[352] Ninety percent of the population of Miami is minority.[353] Between 1980 and 1991, minority representation increased from 15.8 percent of sworn officers to 42 percent in the Metro-Dade Police Department.[354] Director Taylor of Metro-Dade testified that for the last ten years minorities have comprised 70 to 90 percent of each academy class.[355] As of 1990, minorities constituted 70 percent of the population of Dade County.[356]

Between 1983 and 1992, the number of black officers in the Los Angeles Police Department increased by 81.8 percent. African Americans constituted 14 percent of the population in 1990 and 14.3 percent of the LAPD in 1992. In contrast, the number of Hispanic officers in the Los Angeles Police Department increased by only 12.2 percent in the same period. While 39.5 percent of Los Angeles is Hispanic, this group constitutes only 22.3 percent of the city's police force.[357]

Between 1986 and 1991, minority representation in the Indianapolis Police Department increased from 13.9 percent to 17.4 percent.[358] The chief of the Virginia Beach Police Department testified that 12 percent of the force is made up of minorities, an increase of 2 percent over the preceding decade, making the department comparable to the minority population of the city. He also testified that no academy class in the past ten years started with fewer than 25 percent minorities and women.[359] The superintendent of the Missouri State Highway Patrol testified that more minorities had been hired in the last three years than in any comparable period and that they now comprise 6.6 percent of the total workforce and 9.3 percent of the patrol officers.[360] However, the department's definition of "minorities" includes women.[361]

Officials in some cities testified that they were not satisfied with the current number of African American officers in the police department. The vice-mayor of Norfolk testified: "[W]e have an affirmative action plan and it's one of the areas . . . that I am less proud of. We have not been able to get the number of black policemen in the police department . . . that I had hoped that we would have had by this time."[362] Chief Shipley of the Chesapeake police testified his department had tried for a number of years to increase "minority representation," and had been recognized for its efforts, but he was not satisfied with the 13 percent minority representation among sworn personnel.[363] The mayor of Chesapeake testified that, inasmuch as his city had an African American population of 28 percent, there is "room for improvement."[364]

Similarly, a representative from the St. Louis County Police Department testified that "[d]espite an extensive effort to recruit minority applicants for a career in law enforcement the Department has not achieved the level of success that [it] had anticipated."[365] In that police department, 7 percent of commissioned officers are minorities and 6 percent are female, in contrast to a county minority population of 11 percent.[366]

Other departments have made some progress in increasing minority representation, but they still do not nearly reflect the population they serve. In the St. Louis Metropolitan Police Department, 28 percent of the commissioned officers are minorities;[367] in contrast, 47 percent of the city's population is African American.[368] Between 1988 and 1991, the percentage of black commissioned officers in the department increased from 22.8 percent to 27.2 percent.[369] During the same period, 55 percent of the four hundred commissioned officers hired by the St. Louis Metropolitan Police Department were white (48 percent male and 7 percent female), while 44 percent were African American (34.5 percent male and 9.5 percent female).[370] A St. Louis witness stated that, even if the department met its goal of having 50 percent of new officers being minorities, it would take until 2015 or 2020 before the St. Louis Metropolitan Police Department would "be on par with the population."[371]

Minority representation in the Houston Police Department is dismal. While African Americans constitute 28 percent of the city's population, only 15 percent of noncivilian personnel are black.[372] White men constitute 62 percent of Houston's officers, while the city itself has a white population of 44 percent.[373] The chairman of the board of the Afro American Sheriffs Deputies League likened the sheriff's department in the Houston area to apartheid.[374]

Even where overall minority representation has increased in a police department, such growth may be related more to increases in the civilian personnel than in the sworn workforce.[375] Clearly, it is the sworn workforce that is most visible in the community. Interactions between these officers and citizens give rise to the most serious allegations of misconduct. For example, while African Americans constitute 30.4 percent of the Miami Police Department, in a city with a population that is 27.4 percent black, only 20.7 percent of the sworn force is black (53.7 percent of the civilian personnel are black). In contrast, whites make up 34 percent of the sworn ranks, while only 10.1 percent of the population of Miami is white.[376]

Some police representatives described the positive consequences of increased minority representation in their departments. The chief of the Long Beach Police Department testified that affirmative action has been a major influence in changing his organization.[377] The chief of the force in Chesapeake testified that he expected his department's efforts to increase minority recruitment, training, and career development to improve its capability and image and to reduce turnover rates and incidents of misconduct.[378]

6 Finding: African Americans and other minorities are poorly represented in ranks above patrol officer and in the specialized units in many police departments

In the Houston Police Department, white males constitute 97 percent of the captains, 87 percent of the lieutenants, and 81 percent of the sergeants.[379] A Houston policeman testified that of 460 Hispanic officers, there are very few sergeants or lieutenants and no captains.[380] Only 5.3 percent of supervisory positions are held by African Americans, and only 7.8 percent are held by Hispanics.[381]

African Americans constitute 22 percent of the command rank in the St. Louis Metropolitan Police Department,[382] while the city has a black population of more than 47 percent. In the Virginia Beach Police Department, African Americans constituted 8.3 percent of the force in 1992, but only 1.8 percent of those in the supervisory ranks.[383] Even where the overall numbers of minorities in a police department have increased substantially, few African Americans have risen far in the ranks. For example, in the Metro-Dade Police Department only 8.5 percent of the sworn force above the rank of patrolman is black.[384] In the top sixty-five positions, 77 percent are white, 11 percent are black, and 13.8 percent are Hispanic.[385] In the Los Angeles Police Department, the percentage of sworn officers who are African American (14.1 percent) is comparable to the percentage of African Americans in the city's population (14 percent), but only 8.5 percent of the officers in supervisory positions are African Americans. Hispanics, who make up exactly one-third of the population of Los Angeles, constitute 22.2 percent of all sworn officers and 14.3 percent of the supervisors.[386]

Odell McGawan, a St. Louis County commissioner and the first African American to sit on the St. Louis County Police Board, described the need for greater representation of minorities in the supervisory ranks of the St. Louis County Police Department:

> Working within the budget we currently have . . . I'd like to see minorities get a bigger piece of the pie . . . more than two black

sergeants and one Hispanic sergeant [in] . . . a number of 57. I'd like to see more than one black lieutenant in a number of 16. I'd like to see a captain, I'd like to see a major, I'd even like to see a chief.[387]

In some departments—for example, the St. Louis Metropolitan Police Department[388] and the Miami Police Department, and, since the NAACP hearings, Los Angeles and Indianapolis—the chief of police is African American. The Houston department recently had an African American chief of police, who left to become police chief in New York City. While representation of minorities at the highest level of the police department is commendable, it is no substitute for equitable representation throughout the force. The overall representation of minorities in the ranks of patrol officer and in the supervisory ranks is poor.[389] In New York City, the percentage of African Americans in the sworn ranks did not increase between 1983 and 1992, remaining at 11.4 percent, even though the 1990 census found that African Americans comprise 28.7 percent of the population in New York City.[390] The director of a Houston community group testified that, while the former African American chief of police had a different and better concept of policing and was more open to complaints by citizens, "the problem is more systemic, and brutality can even increase with a black Chief—due to the illusion of fairness."[391]

Some police officials testified that local laws hinder affirmative action for recruits and intermediate commanding officers. For example, in the Houston Police Department promotions are based solely on seniority and a multiple-choice test.[392] The mayor of Houston testified that "[n]othing is allowed to be taken into account about performance, leadership ability or anything else."[393] She also testified that it is against Texas law for police or fire departments to have an affirmative action program as part of their process for promotions.[394] "That has resulted in it taking a very long time to remedy the traditional discrimination that has occurred in decades past, in the advancement of ethnic minorities in our police department and our fire department. That's something that needs to be changed."[395] In contrast, the Houston Police Department has an affirmative action program for civilian personnel "that has allowed for better ethnic representation and diversification in that area."[396] A task force has been authorized to improve the system of promotion and to include performance and a verbal assessment as factors to be considered.[397]

Minorities are also underrepresented in the specialized units of many police departments, positions that are often considered desirable. There are no African Americans in the internal affairs division in the Houston[398] or St. Louis County Police Departments.[399] A witness in the latter city testified that there are few African Americans in the specialized units (including homicide, narcotics, fraud, and arson) in the St. Louis Metropolitan Police Department, at least in part because they have not had equal opportunities to receive specialized academy training.[400]

Some departments have adapted their policies to increase the number of minorities eligible for promotion. The St. Louis County Police Department amended its written examination and dropped the requirement of a bachelor's degree for promotion to lieutenant or captain.[401] As a result, the number of applicants eligible for promotion increased by 30 percent.[402] In Houston, successful efforts were made to change state law to allow for "diverse ethnic representation in the highest command levels.''[403] The Metro-Dade Police Department created two new ranks, master sergeant and first lieutenant, as a "way to increase minority participation.''[404] The Chesapeake Police Department has established an "alternative career path" that allows officers who do not want to become supervisors to increase their professional status and pay without competing for promotions.[405] The chief of operations in the Norfolk Police Department testified, "[I]t's a business necessity to have, say, a minority, or female, or black supervisor in certain communities to deal with certain problems. . . .''[406] Recognizing the lack of African American officers in particular ranks, this department also developed plans to allow officers to increase their pay and prestige without applying for promotions.[407]

G Police Departments Are Beginning to Respond to the Needs of the Community in Police Training Programs

1 Finding: Police departments are beginning to require basic training in cultural diversity

Citizens, police representatives, and elected officials testified that police officers should receive training in cultural sensitivity and violence reduction in order to improve police-community relations.[408] One citizen, expressing her concern about the lack of such training for officers, testified: "[M]uch of their time is spent putting us in jail as opposed to understanding that we're a decent kind of people. They always want to stop us and find out who we are."[409] The mayor of Miami testified that "some officers, who have not been in that community, do not know that particular ethnic group and react in a particular way and that is a concern of extensive training."[410]

Most of the police departments represented at the hearings have instituted some kind of training on these topics.[411] However, there is a great deal of variety in the focus of the respective departments on basic and in-service training in these issues.

An official of the St. Louis County Police Department testified that state law requires 600 hours of training, 40 of which are devoted to work on cultural awareness. The training includes topics like "sensitivity in minority communities" and uses role-playing techniques.[412] Recruits in the St. Louis Metropolitan Police Department receive 40 hours of human relations training,[413] while 30 of the 1,000 hours of basic training for the Missouri State Highway Patrol are devoted to "policing in America," described by a police official as dealing primarily with cultural awareness.[414] Chief Ross of Miami testified that 50 of 820 hours of basic training are dedicated to cultural awareness, sensitivity, and community relations.[415] In the Metro-Dade Police Department, 120 of 700 hours of basic training focus on dealing with violence.[416]

Matthew Hunt, a deputy chief in the Los Angeles department, testified that in the aftermath of the Rodney King incident, the LAPD had extended basic training at the academy from six to seven months and was "concentrating on addressing such issues as culture awareness, respect for the individual, use of force, [and] discipline. . . ."[417] Deputy Chief Hunt testified that the six months of training at the academy was "barely adequate to take care of the complexities in our society today.[418]

Cadet training in the Houston Police Department includes sixteen hours of work on "cultural awareness."[419] Chief Watson testified that classes in cultural awareness and sensitivity by themselves are not sufficient, even when followed by field training; it is important to have officers "out in the community, learning firsthand what the community cares about." Her department is "completely revising" the training curriculum to bring community representatives into the classroom to "share their experiences."[420]

Clearly, short-term training in cultural awareness and sensitivity, though a step in the right direction, does not guarantee that new officers will be respectful to minority citizens and will refrain from misconduct, particularly if they work in a climate of prejudice and hostility toward minorities (whether minority officers or citizens).[421] Miami's chief of police testified that ongoing retraining in cultural awareness, after experience on the street, will have a greater impact on officers than will courses at the police academy.[422] The president of the Houston Police Organization of Spanish Speaking Officers, referring to what he viewed as an "excellent" class on cultural differences, testified:

> [T]he attitude of the class was hostile. These attitudes . . . take a long time to form. . . . [O]ne day of training out of seventeen and a half years I have been in the department is insufficient. . . . Discrimination has taken on a new face. It has become very sophisticated . . . by using the rules as our manuals to go ahead and allow them to exclude minorities from upward mobility.[423]

2 Finding: Some police departments have instituted in-service cultural diversity training

Some police departments have also made cultural awareness, diversity, and violence reduction part of in-service training.[424] Chief Ross of Miami testified that the department had no in-house training programs in sensitivity or cultural awareness in 1980,[425] a situation that has since been remedied. For example, some Miami police attend community relations seminars at a local black college.[426] All Miami officers are required to attend "street wisdom" training, which addresses community concerns and ways in which the police can improve communication with and services to the multiethnic community.[427] The Miami Police Department has participated in "Kingian" nonviolence instruction for the past few years; the program is designed to teach persons to conduct in-house training in nonviolent conflict resolution.[428] The department in Miami also has an eight-hour "ethnic sharing program" aimed at fostering respect for differences among the officers themselves.[429]

In the Metro-Dade department, the following training is given: stress awareness and resolution (40 hours); crisis intervention (40 hours); human and community relations (40 hours); investment in excellence (40 hours), required for all recruits, which "teaches officers to approach problems in a positive manner" and encourages them "to view situations through the eyes of the people that they encounter"; Police Effective Awareness Key (PEAK), relating to conflict and criticism, supervisory responsibilities, and officer survival techniques (16 hours); alternatives to use of force (8 hours); and violence reduction training (40 hours).[430] In Houston, plans were being made for 20 hours of cultural awareness training each year.[431] The new chief of the St. Louis Metropolitan Police Department testified that his department began an intensive cultural diversity training program in 1991 (participation is mandatory for all members of the force, from patrol officers to the chief), as part of the annual in-service training.[432]

Some departments have called on "outside experts" to provide or supervise training on cultural awareness issues.[433] The Chesapeake Police Department uses a "minority team" of outside experts to assist with sensitivity training.[434] In the Houston Police Department, outside experts have been used for supervisory training, and the Anti-Defamation League gives cultural awareness and sensitivity training that also focuses on the gay and lesbian community.[435] However, there was criticism of the choice of experts to give the sensitivity training, since they did not come from the affected minority communities.[436]

Miami's "street wisdom training" is taught by the National Conference of Christians and Jews, and the "ethnic sharing" program is conducted by the American Jewish Committee. The National Organization of Black Law Enforcement Executives has also provided training in conflict resolution to Miami police officers.[437]

While many of the police officials described the number of hours devoted to "human relations," "cultural awareness," or "sensitivity" training (whether basic or in-service), there was little testimony regarding the substance of the training itself. The Florida Law Enforcement Basic Recruit Training Course materials describe a 520-hour program, which includes 25 hours of "interpersonal training." Of these 25 hours, 4 hours are devoted to crisis intervention techniques, 5 hours to stress recognition and reduction, 4 hours to interpersonal skills, and 2 hours to human behavior/human needs. Only 2 hours are given to "ethnic and cultural groups," with the stated goal of this part of the course being to "know the concepts of ethnic and cultural groups and comprehend how the values, customs, and behavior of different ethnic and cultural groups affect the performance of an officer's duties." The remainder of the 25 hours deals with problems of juveniles, persons with mental illness, persons with mental retardation, abusers of alcohol and other drugs, the physically handicapped, and the elderly. While all of these topics are important areas to address in training, the limited amount of time devoted to "ethnic and cultural groups"—2 hours out of 25—raises questions about whether issues of race, class, and gender are being adequately addressed.[438]

H Racism Has a Detrimental Effect on Law Enforcement

Shelby Lanier, chairman of the National Black Police Association, emphasized how race poisons the relationship between the police and the community:

> There is no place in the law enforcement profession for police brutality, misuse of authority, or oppressive racism. Those who commit these actions endanger the lives of those few public servants who attempt to do the right thing while exercising the privilege of being a police officer. . . . Government has failed nationally and locally to stop this trend. Nor have allegations, revelations, and investigations been adequate deterrents to those involved and responsible.[439]

The Christopher Commission noted that a survey conducted by the Los Angeles Police Department after the King beating found that approximately one-quarter of the respondents, all sworn officers, agreed that "racial bias on the part of officers toward minority citizens currently exists and contributes to a negative interaction between police and the community." Similarly, 27.6 percent agreed that "an officer's prejudice towards the suspect's race may lead to the use of excessive force."[440]

Minority police officers live with racism every day.[441] Intradepartmental racism has a concrete effect on their treatment and acceptance within the department and on the way officers interact with the public. When radio messages include racial slurs and comments against minority officers, it is no wonder police officers treat black citizens badly. The failure of police departments to enforce internal regulations against racism greatly increases the power of a relatively small number of overtly racist police. When those in charge allow day-to-day derogation to occur, regular officers are discouraged from reporting such incidents.[442] When officers are discouraged from reporting these events within their own department, it inevitably makes police officers reluctant to report abuse of the population at large.[443]

The "war on crime" and the "war on drugs" have encouraged selective and racist law enforcement. In the name of eradicating drugs, police have been given a free hand to harass, violate the rights of, and brutalize minority groups. In the name of crime control, the police have reduced all African Americans to criminals.

John W. Mack, of the Urban League of Los Angeles, stated that some in the minority community look the other way while police abuse is taking place:

I think we've reached the point in trying to come to grips with the drug problem, the gang problem, all the problems of violence that really do have most African American communities under siege, whether in Los Angeles or another city, we find ourself [*sic*] being held hostage to this problem. And we have the situation where police departments such as Los Angeles Police Department have been given free license to disregard people's basic civil liberties within the problem of going after the gangs and the drugs, and people turn their heads the other way.[444]

In this atmosphere, police have become as likely to turn on law-abiding citizens as on those who violate the law. As a result, ordinary people are warning their children about the police. Average African American families do not know whether they should call the police, stop for the police, or help the police—all for fear of becoming a target of police misconduct themselves.[445]

A witness in Norfolk stated: "What the police do and how they do it impacts on community relations: recruitment, retention, morale and conduct. Community instability and lack of respect for officers can result in assaults or killing of officers."[446] Rickie Clark, a member of the National Black Police Association, describes the impact of police brutality on the attitude of law-abiding citizens and on law enforcement:

Police brutality is a vital issue because it certainly undermines the basic crime control function of a police officer. The police must have cooperation from its citizens in reporting crime and giving evidence in order to control crime. Brutality . . . leads the people to fear and distrust the police as much as the criminal. The citizen[s'] cooperation—that is absolutely essential in fighting crime, will never be forthcoming while police brutality continues.[447]

Herman E. Springs, director of police at Norfolk State University, pointed out that community-police relations and confidence in the police on the part of the community are at an all-time low.[448] A number of witnesses talked about having lost their respect for the police. Several said that, if they needed help, they would hesitate before calling the police.[449] Deborah Gordon put it poignantly: "How can I [have respect] when they killed my son?"[450]

Police abuse in all forms undermines cooperation from the community. It is unlikely, for example, that Wanda Gonzalez, a witness at the Miami hearings, will be forthcoming in cooperating with the police in the future. Ms. Gonzalez stated that, as a community leader in a minority neighborhood, she tries "to get the police department and the neighborhood together."[451] She described an event in the early morning hours as she was supervising some neighborhood kids. A police officer appeared, cursed her and others around her, and called them "animals, chickens, . . . a bunch of creeps."[452]

The isolation of the police from minority communities only serves to foster bad attitudes and ineffective police work. Several of the law-enforcement personnel testified that they understood that the police department could not afford to define itself as an entity apart from the community. Commenting on ways to become "closer related to the community," Chief Ian Shipley testified, "[W]e readily realize that the effectiveness of any social service agency is to understand the problem and this understanding must flow through the entire organization from the top to the bottom and maybe more importantly from the bottom to the top."[453]

FINDINGS

Herman E. Springs, director of police at Norfolk State University, believes that confronting police abuse and brutality as the acts are occurring is the most effective approach. In his experience, disarming and arresting officers on the street works.[454] For him, it is imperative that black officers let the community know that they will not tolerate misconduct by other police officers.[455]

The minority community finds itself in the middle of a very troubling situation. While many abhor the violence and gang-related activity that is taking place among them, many also find it difficult to support a police department that seems to lump everyone, good and bad, together. There are consequences for the future of young black people. Mafundi Jitahadi of Los Angeles described the effect of police overreaction on employment:

> A youth is arrested because he is wearing a Raider's cap or a Raider jacket and fits a so-called gang profile. He is pulled over, detained, and then afterwards released, and his name is entered into a database tracking system. Later on when this youth is applying for employment, the employer can pull this out and see that he was detained as a gangbanger and does refuse him employment, thus maybe forcing him into the underground economy.[456]

There must be a new emphasis on community relations and mutual respect. As a witness in Indianapolis testified: "Unemployment, poverty, drugs, crime and violence are community problems. These problems must be addressed with the community oriented attitude, community oriented solutions, community oriented policing. [A] [m]ilitary at war [with] the community attitude must end."[457]

At present, community relations do not appear to be an institutional priority for most police departments. As Matthew Hunt, deputy chief of the Los Angeles Police Department, commented:

> There is a very, very small portion of the budget that is devoted to community relations, very, very small. . . . [I]n most of our eighteen divisions across the city, you will find perhaps two or three people that are working full time in supporting the community relations operation.[458]

In the final analysis, the police know that if they are serious about reducing crime in the "inner city," they cannot do it without the help of the community. The community wants to help, but is increasingly distrustful of the police. It is incumbent on law enforcement to win back the trust of the citizens they serve.

Cynics might respond that the police have no interest in putting resources into community relations in the inner city. As long as inner-city crime does not spill over into the nice areas of town, the police are willing to go along with business as usual. However, police and the minority communities have the power to change this perception. A new bond of cooperation must be cultivated. As Deputy Chief Hunt said: "The police department cannot police the city on its own. If we do not have the support and the active participation of the community, we are not going to be able to do the job."[459]

RECOMMENDATIONS FOR CHANGE

A There Must Be Sweeping Change in the Concept of Policing

1 "Us versus them" dynamic must change

There must be serious change in the very concept of policing in our cities and towns. The first change must be to do away with the "us versus them" dynamic of police-community relations. This drawing of lines—and more, this taking of sides—only fosters racism and violence, and it needs to be altered.[1]

There was much testimony throughout the NAACP hearings on the police being outside or above the community.[2] There was much testimony about an insular police culture that disparages all outsiders, particularly those in minority communities.[3] There was considerable testimony by members of the African American community about the racial animosity that is part and parcel of the "us versus them" mentality.[4]

The sides as drawn hold the police out as the good guys and everyone else—especially those of color—as the bad guys. This is the sort of outlook that fosters police disregard of the constitutional rights of young black people. This is the sort of value system that spawns police perjury. This is the ideology that fosters an apartheid-like experience for all African Americans in the inner city. Paradoxically, the "us versus them" view held by so many officers fosters the kind of anger and hostility toward the police that leads to violence directed against them and to police killings.

We recognize that changing the conception of the police as an occupying force in the community will not happen easily or quickly.[5] There is no single program that can be instituted or policy that can be adopted that in and of itself can transform the nature of police-community relations. The commitment to change must be made at all levels in the police department and in local and national government.[6] It must be demonstrated concretely throughout police department policies, practices, and programs. Efforts to improve police-community relations must receive both financial and moral support from elected government. Similarly, it will take an ongoing, active effort to participate in finding solutions to collective problems, whether as part of the police force or as residents of the community.[7]

2 Police officers must be part of the community they serve

Police officers must integrate themselves into the community.[8] The presence of outsiders with weapons, policing a community they neither know nor understand, perpetuates the notion of police officers as an occupying army. Roots in the community, or at least a commitment to developing roots, must be seen as an important hiring criterion.[9]

A witness in Houston described the reasons for police to be part of the community:

> [M]any of the policemen do not live in [the] City of Houston. And that is part of the problem. Even when I was growing up, I did

know all the policemen. . . . And they lived in the neighborhood, and we knew them. And we also—we knew that we could get in trouble with them, and they would also come to our parents and say whatever they thought about the kids' behavior. But the policeman [sic] today have no connection and no relationship with the neighborhood.[10]

Though the idea is in some aspects controversial, we join a number of those who testified at the hearings in strongly recommending that officers be required to live within a short commuting distance from where they work.[11] A number of police departments have some sort of residency requirement.[12] If police officers reside in or near the neighborhoods in which they work, they will come to know the other residents as people.[13] Once they come to know their neighbors, they will find both similarity and difference. They will be forced to acknowledge the humanity of those whom they police. In addition, there might be a corollary benefit to blighted inner-city neighborhoods in maintaining a pool of middle-class residents.

We also recommend that police officers be required, as part of their job, to participate in community-related endeavors.[14] There are an infinite number of choices: public school activities; recreational sports programs; the Girl and Boy Scouts; the Big Brother/Big Sister program; teenage pregnancy centers; drug rehabilitation programs; centers for the elderly; women's centers; rape crisis offices; gay and lesbian rights centers; AIDS hotlines and programs; classes in English as a second language; immigrant centers; programs for the physically disabled; offices for the mentally ill; and centers for the mentally retarded.

3   Police officers must be reconceptualized as social service providers

Police officers must be reconceptualized as public servants engaged in social service delivery.[15] Notwithstanding their current paramilitary image and structure,[16] this was the original conceptualization of the police.[17] Officers have always been urban "helpers," providing information, directing other municipal services to areas of need, and serving as an essential neighborhood resource.[18]

The stereotype of the police function as catching criminals and fighting crime has always reflected only a small part of the police role. The stereotype is firmly planted in the minds of both law-enforcement officers and the general public, and it has been cultivated by the police themselves. This is the "Lethal Weapon" image of police in America; it pervades our popular culture in books, on television, and at the movies.[19] This image has an enormous influence on the organization, staffing, and operation of police agencies.[20]

While crime fighting will always be an important part of police work,[21] it is not the only police function, nor is it necessarily the most important one.[22] In inner-city areas, police perform the widest array of services. Here, the combination of poverty, unemployment, dilapidated housing, poor education, and homelessness results in police officers being called on to serve as

surrogate parent or other relative, and to fill in for social workers, housing inspectors, attorneys, physicians, and psychiatrists. It is here, too, that the police most frequently care for those who cannot care for themselves: the destitute, the inebriated, the addicted, the mentally ill, the senile, the alien, the physically disabled, and the very young.[23]

Why not reconceptualize the police as part of the "Urban Corps," an inner-city version of the Peace Corps? Other members of the corps could include firefighters, social workers, community mental health professionals, health care providers, public school teachers, drug and alcohol addiction counselors, and youth counselors.[24] The "Urban Corps" could focus on long-term, multidisciplinary solutions to crime, polarization, and urban decay.[25] One rarely, if ever, hears of widespread tension between the community and firefighters. No doubt the reason is that firefighters are seen as providing an essential service, without taking anything from the community. Citizens are not afraid of them.

Police officers must, at the same time, be reconceptualized as important, valuable members of the community, essential to a free society. Police should be seen as the keepers of the calm, the keepers of safety. What could be a more important social role? Police ought to be compensated for their work to an extent commensurate with its value.[26] Revaluing police work ought to be part of a massive rethinking of a number of undervalued occupations, such as public school teaching, public health care provision, and legal representation of indigent people.

B There Must Be Greater Police Accountability

Effective management of any large bureaucracy requires systematic, formalized, and comprehensive mechanisms to ensure attainment of the organization's goals and objectives. Among the most important are mechanisms to achieve *accountability*—rewarding and encouraging positive police behavior, as well as preventing, mitigating, and improving negative police performance.

This may be more important for the police bureaucracy than for any other because the police "are given special powers, unique in our society, to use force, even deadly force, in the furtherance of their duties."[27] As enforcers of the law, they are not only an agent of the values our society deems most important, they are the most visible barrier between civilized society and its alternatives.

It is axiomatic that "the right to use force carries with it a heavy responsibility not to abuse it."[28] When armed law enforcers engage in use of excessive force, abuse of power, or "merely" rude or discourteous behavior, the injury is not only to individual citizens but to the Constitution, our sense of community, and our collective sense of dignity.[29]

In a time of enormous social change—in racial and ethnic composition, economic direction, family structure, suburban-urban relationships, and the role of government—we must be especially vigilant to uphold, and not to take for granted, the social balance of power. Police must serve the community; community members must not become the servants, tools, or whipping boys (and girls) of the police.

It is essential that those at the top, police leaders and managers, devise control mechanisms that work. It is also essential that

> leadership . . . be comprehensive and constant, not isolated or sporadic. They must make their weight felt throughout the

system—from recruitment, through training, promotion, assignment, and discipline. . . . To make genuine progress on issues relating to excessive force, racism, and bias, leadership must avoid sending mixed signals. . . . Leniency in discipline or easy forgiveness . . . will be misread as condoning improper practices.[30]

The leadership of the police department must make clear both the rules of conduct and the consequences for violation of the rules, whether the misconduct is by actual behavior, by ignoring the improper conduct of other officers, or by failing to supervise.[31]

1   Goals, objectives, and priorities

Goals and priorities must be defined as clearly and comprehensively as possible, including the expansive mission of the police, law-enforcement values, and an overriding respect for human dignity. These must be fully and unequivocally adopted by the highest levels of the department, as well as by the government, which controls the department and is directly accountable to the community.

Our society has increasingly, and mistakenly, looked to the police to solve the complex problems of our time. These problems cannot be solved by policing alone. Thus, the department's official values and goals must also encompass "learning to say 'no' in ways that educate and enlighten, for communities and groups will ask things of the police which the police ought not to do, and the police must learn how to instruct the public about limits and tolerance."[32]

Thus, for the first step, it is imperative that all the goals, objectives, guidelines, and rules—for all levels of the department—be spelled out clearly, in detail, and *in writing*.[33] These must not simply be inscribed in manuals, bound and buried, but must be distributed to everyone involved in police work. Moreover, the goals and guidelines of policing must be explicitly referred to by those in command, on a regular basis, in every context.

A preliminary list of specific rules that bear particular examination—or adoption, if not in existence—includes: (1) rules defining permissible uses of various levels of force, particularly deadly force, and rules prohibiting excessive force; (2) rules defining and forbidding racism, sexism, violations of constitutional rights, and other forms of misconduct; (3) rules imposing liability on sworn officers who are "nonparticipatory bystanders"[34] at the scene of misconduct by other officers; and (4) rules pertaining to disciplinary proceedings, such as sanctions for discouraging or deterring the filing of complaints, or for following the code of silence.

2   Screening, hiring, and training

Entry-level and in-service screening, hiring, and training of police must not only reflect the values and goals of police departments, they must be designed to fully attain them. Accordingly, police departments must be willing and able to screen for and reject from service those who lack sufficient respect for law, recruits who would likely be unable to uphold the law in the face of deep-seated personal feelings to the contrary.

Tendencies toward bias, uncontrolled temper, and violence may have to become, per se, grounds for disqualification. Respect for law, fairness, and decency may have to become more important criteria for service than physical or intellectual fitness.

3 Performance appraisal, evaluation, and accountability

Personnel evaluation policies and systems must be designed to comprehensively ensure that all levels of the department fully attain specified values, goals, and objectives and comply with guidelines, rules, and policies.

A recent article by Geoffrey P. Alpert and Mark H. Moore is a good starting point for police management interested in rethinking police accountability. The article, "Measuring Police Performance in the New Paradigm of Policing,"[35] argues that the traditional measures of police performance—reported crime rates, overall arrests, clearance rates, and response times—are outmoded. While these aspects of policing should continue to be regarded as critical parts of the overall system, "[p]olice performance measures should focus on a new model of policing that emphasizes their charge to do justice, promote secure communities, restore crime victims, and promote non-criminal options—the elements of an emerging paradigm of criminal justice."[36]

According to Alpert and Moore, policing in America has been guided by a vision of professionalism that is no longer effective in reducing crime or the public's fear of crime. Police "professionalism" has led to distancing of the police from those who need their services most. The heart of the paradigm proposed in the article is that police "engage in community-based processes related to the production and maintenance of local human and social capital."[37] In order to do this, police departments must build strong relationships with institutions and individuals in the community.

Alpert and Moore suggest that police professionalism should be reflected in audited clearance and arrest rates and the development of statistical evidence on the use of force and the incidence of brutality. New, community-centered performance measures would include the level of decentralization of a department and the number of community-level programs it oversees. Measures would also include police and governmental activities that improve the social fabric of the community, police projects undertaken in conjunction with private industry that improve social control in the community, a decrease in the fear of crime, and programs for crime victims and others in need of police services that help promote community spirit where none had existed.[38]

The article provides specific examples of successful systems in urban areas and offers suggestions about neighborhood training, monitoring, and rewarding of individual officers.[39]

In concurrence with these views, we specifically recommend:

a Periodic, systematic performance evaluations

The performance of personnel must be measured against previously set, strict standards. Evaluations should occur regularly, at least once a year, and more often where merited.

b Revised criteria for evaluation

The lack of a history of complaints by civilians, a demonstrated ability to use means other than force to control a police situation, skill at de-escalating a potentially violent encounter, skill at steering addicted persons into treatment instead of the criminal justice system, work in the community to prevent gang membership, and a demonstrated capacity for both professionalism and sympathy in responding to hate crimes ought to be criteria for a positive evaluation.[40] A history of complaints, excessive force, and involvement in minor street encounters that escalate to physical confrontations and arrests should be criteria for a negative evaluation. All criteria should reflect the high aims of the department.

c New and creative ways to reward and reinforce positive behavior should be devised

Though the primary system of rewards and punishments will undoubtedly continue to be promotions and job security, the commonly used rewards of "commendation" and reassignment to more desirable positions should be broadened in scope. New devices, like longevity pay for patrol functions, should be adopted.[41]

d There should be a formalized personnel appraisal system

Most police departments have formalized personnel systems. Boston's St. Clair Commission reported that "only *four* of the 31 major urban police departments do not have a formalized personnel system."[42] Officers at all levels must be periodically and officially evaluated for their performance, including their supervisory performance, if any. Supervisors should be held accountable for the conduct of those under their control, and they must be supported when they take action against those who engage in improper conduct.[43] Methods of *monitoring* behavior must be devised, including such techniques as "spot-checks," "sting" operations, community focus groups,[44] and input from both community groups and citizen surveys.[45]

e Complaints that are "not sustained" should be included in personnel files and factored in if a pattern of complaints is found

Whatever disciplinary system is adopted for complaints and allegations of misconduct, it is important that complaints classified as "not sustained" or "unfounded" or that are for some reason withdrawn or dismissed be retained in personnel files, particularly if there is a "pattern."[46] Consideration should be given to making such a history available in future investigations of the same officer—or of the officer's supervisor.[47] Such a pattern should be factored into overall performance appraisal, and it should be grounds for corrective steps and/or discipline.[48]

f No level of the police department should be exempt from evaluation

The chief of police, and all of those in leadership roles, must also be formally evaluated on a regular basis by an objective body answerable to the appointing authority. High-ranking officers must hold their jobs with a delicately balanced combination of independence and accountability.[49] Police chiefs and elected leaders must make clear both the principles and the policies they expect the police to follow.[50]

g Departments must keep systematic records of police-community interaction on racial and ethnic lines

All police departments should begin to institute systematic record-keeping procedures that will keep track of racial and ethnic categories in stops, arrests, and physical confrontations between police and civilians. While the hearings provided overwhelming evidence that African Americans, Hispanics, and other minority ethnic groups are disproportionately subjected to more police intrusion and abuse, statistical documentation of this is woefully lacking. It is time for local police departments—and the United States Department of Justice—to start collecting the kind of hard facts this country needs to address the issue of race and police meaningfully.

4 Civil service laws need to be reevaluated

Civil service laws are troubling—and controversial—in the context of police accountability. In many places, they appear to be inflexible and outmoded.[51] They must either be replaced or drastically revised, with more sophisticated combinations of limited job security and insulation from political influence, on the one hand, and objective appraisal systems providing accountability to the community, on the other.[52]

C There Must Be a Real Commitment to Diversity in Hiring

1 Police departments should reflect the communities they serve

There is no question that police officers should be more like the communities they serve, a recommendation made by many who testified at the NAACP hearings throughout the country.[53] Almost all the police officials who testified at these hearings presented their department's affirmative action plan, emphasizing successes in recruiting, hiring, and promotions, and apologetically explaining the failures. There was an almost universal view that diversity in the police ranks was a key to bettering police-minority relations[54] and to stopping police brutality.[55]

There are a number of concerns, however. First, the picture of a wholly black police force in wholly black neighborhoods perpetuates racial segregation on every level.[56] The Rodney King incident and the unrest that followed were not unrelated to Los Angeles's status as one of the most racially segregated cities in the United States.[57]

Second, there is something a bit worrisome about black expansion in police hirings in the last twenty years as compared to other occupations. Between 1970 and 1990, African Americans took 41.4 percent of new police positions.[58] In that same period, blacks took only 7.4 percent of new pharmacist positions, 10.1 percent of new health official positions, and 12.7 percent of new electrician positions.[59] Policing is quite literally a blue-collar job. Policing also has a very public profile, and is increasingly associated with the black "underclass" that is so heavily policed.

While affirmative action plans and a serious commitment to diversity in the police must be part of any recommendation for change,[60] affirmative action and diversity are not a panacea. Police culture runs deep.[61] While the figures seem to show that police officers of color tend to commit fewer acts of police brutality, and less severe forms of it,[62] it is not true that African American officers never assault or abuse African American citizens.[63]

It has not seemed to matter historically that police officers tend to come from the working class: when confronted with a choice of identifying with that class or carrying out their duties as police officers in a way that was destructive to members of the working class, the police always identified as police.[64] Why do we think that African American police officers, when confronted with a conflict in identity—African American or police—would see themselves as African American first? Will they profit from that identification professionally? Personally? In a society that devalues and degrades African American identity, why would a police officer embrace that identity first?

Central to police culture is a dichotomy: "us versus them." There is nothing complex about the line drawing. It is not "some-of-us versus them" or even "most-of-us versus them." There may be a cost to African American police officers who dare to be African American first. A commitment to a diverse police force must be accompanied by a commitment to changing police culture.

2 Police leadership must be more diverse

Most police departments have done better with bringing minorities and women into the force at the bottom levels than in promoting minorities and women to positions of leadership and power.[65] Diversity in police leadership is essential to changing the face of policing.[66]

D Police Departments Must Evaluate Criteria for Recruitment and Hiring

1 Police departments should recruit better-educated candidates

Recruiting better-educated persons to be police officers is often suggested as a way of bringing in people with broader perspectives.[67] The broader the educational background, the fuller and broader the perspective. A background in the humanities and the social sciences may give a new police officer a head start in understanding the life circumstances of the people he or she polices.[68]

There is a potential conflict in creating higher education standards for police officers and recruiting police officers from inner-city communities. The schooling received by those born and raised in the inner city is generally not as good as that received by those raised elsewhere. Drop-out rates are also considerably higher in the inner city.[69]

A solution may be to create "conditional employment" arrangements with candidates who are otherwise qualified, but who are lagging behind in education. These candidates would be required to complete their studies as part of their employment contract. The police department would structure the new officers' duties to include their academic work and would provide a supportive atmosphere.[70]

Encouragement and incentives to obtain further education should be part of every police force. Police officers should receive some sort of acknowledgment for further studies in related fields: criminology, criminal justice, sociology, political science, language studies.

2   A special effort should be made to recruit candidates who are less potentially violent

Every police department represented in the NAACP hearings requires recruits to undergo psychological testing. The testing is not elaborate, but, rather, tends to be a standard psychological test.

We join with those who recommend extensive psychological testing for potential violence, intolerance of difference, racism, sexism, and homophobia.[71] We recommend that the testing include more than a written "exam," and that simulations be developed and incorporated into the screening process. Questionnaires should be devised to determine applicants' motivation for becoming police officers. Each applicant should be investigated to determine whether he or she has any history of violence against intimates and family members. It is widely known that there is a high incidence of battering (of wives and girlfriends) by male police officers. Each applicant should be investigated to determine whether he or she has a hidden agenda in joining the force.[72] Careful investigation should determine whether the applicant has the requisite maturity to become a police officer.[73]

3   Hiring police officers free of race, gender, and sexual-orientation bias should be a priority

Police departments should actively seek out and hire police officers who are free of bias. This includes recruiting and hiring greater numbers of African Americans and other minorities, women, and "out" gays and lesbians.[74] A significant part of psychological testing should address bias, and questionnaires modeled after those employed by the National Jury Project to select less biased jurors should be used.[75] Preference should be given to police recruits with racially mixed residential, educational, or employment backgrounds.

4 Police departments must aggressively recruit from the minority community

Police departments vary in how aggressively and creatively they recruit.[76] Houston, for example, conducts nationwide recruiting, retains an advertising agency, and uses mass media.[77] College campuses and military bases are targeted.[78] The St. Louis County Police Department targets black colleges and universities and churches.[79] Chesapeake, Virginia, recruits by advertising in black newspapers, sending speakers to local radio stations, attending traditionally black job fairs, and going to black colleges. The Virginia Beach Police Department has worked with local chapters of the NAACP and churches, while the department in Norfolk has worked with the Urban League.[80]

Police departments should learn from the tactics of military recruiting. They should recruit everywhere: in high schools as well as colleges, in shopping districts, at recreational centers, at ball fields, at the local basketball courts, at "options counseling" sessions for teenage girls, at the Boy and Girl Scouts, at places where gangs hang out. Departments should use sophisticated and clever media campaigns. They should offer incentives to join the police, like money for further education, computer and other technological skills training, scholarship funds for the children of police officers.

E It Is Essential to Offer Continuing Training and Education

Professional schooling must extend beyond the police academy.[81] If multicultural understanding and alternatives to violence are taught only to new recruits, what they learn will be quickly undone after contact with other officers.[82] In police departments that maintain a crime control orientation and do not encourage positive community interaction, too often the stress of police work combines with constant exposure to an "us versus them" mentality within the department to supplant whatever understanding of diversity might be taught at the academy.[83]

The training should include programs that are "clinical" in nature, employing educational methods that include role-plays, simulations, and interactive exercises.[84] The simulations should involve children, families, and neighborhoods of diverse backgrounds. There should be an interdisciplinary team of teachers/trainers to offer feedback on performances.

1 Multicultural sensitivity and understanding should be interwoven into every aspect of training

Multicultural education must be integrated into every part of the training and the ongoing educational program.[85] Most police officials who testified at the NAACP hearings were able to quantify the hours or credits given to "sensitivity training" and multiculturalism.[86] This suggests that sensitivity to diversity is seen as a separate topic, like having one class on black history in a semester course in American history.

As policing occurs in a context of diversity, that context must be part of every lecture, every presentation, every discussion. Efforts should be made to gather a diverse staff of teachers and trainers, so that different voices are heard in the front of the class and so that police officers see talented people of color and women in positions of authority.

2 Teachers and trainers should come from within and without the police to provide a number of perspectives

Those who conduct teaching sessions for the police should come from academia, the minority community, the feminist community, the gay and lesbian community, the religious community, and from among those who work with the homeless, the mentally ill, the drug and alcohol addicted, the battered.

3 Education sessions should be held with other urban social service providers whenever possible

The insularity of the police and other aspects of police culture might be altered by exposure to the perspectives of others serving the same urban population. The hypothesis is that the more views a police officer hears in the course of training and ongoing education, the less likely it is that he or she will conform to a singular "police view."

There are a number of issues that could be taught to groups of police officers, firefighters, social workers, community mental health workers, public hospital workers, public defenders, and district attorneys in a single setting. Each group would benefit from exposure to the others.

F Promotion and Advancement Criteria Must Be Reevaluated

Standards for advancement and promotion should include a history of nonviolent police intervention, the lack of civilian complaints, ongoing educational achievement, ties to the community, and demonstrated efforts to build community. Preference should be given to those who either come from or made themselves part of the community.

G A Community-Oriented Policing Approach Should Be Adopted by All Police Departments

Every police department represented at the NAACP hearings referred to its commitment to "community-oriented policing."[87] Norfolk calls its program PACE (Police Assistance Community Enforcement),[88] while the program established by the St. Louis Metropolitan Police Department is called COPS (Community Oriented Policing Services).[89] The Miami and Metro-Dade Police Departments have a number of programs, all considered some form of "community policing."

Along with many who testified at the hearings, we strongly recommend a community-oriented approach to policing.[90] We applaud those police departments that have embraced such an approach, and we encourage them to continue the work. The problem with efforts so far is that they appear to be piecemeal and extraordinary, rather than integrated into the scheme of the entire policing enterprise.[91]

Community policing is a radically different approach to

crime and other urban problems from what we think of as "traditional" policing.[92] Community policing seeks to address not only crime but *fear*, perhaps an even more crippling societal epidemic.[93] It also seeks to address such diffuse social problems as community and racial tension.[94]

Between the deep-seated causes of crime on the one hand and serious, violent crime on the other "lies a vast world of mundane friction and hurt."[95] This is where fear, tension, and community disorder take root and grow:

> Disorder and neglect—aggressive, drunken panhandlers, threatening youths, walls sullied by gang graffiti—often seem to signal that an area has been abandoned to the forces of decline, and can be an even stronger trigger for fear than crime itself. Disputes—inside families, between landlords and tenants, employers and employees, black and white neighborhood basketball teams, delivery drivers and other road users—can cut at the fabric of social and community life and often develop into assaults and other crimes. Social and medical emergencies—runaways, the homeless, the dangerously ill clothed and ill fed—are serious on their own merits and frequently lead to victimization and crime.[96]

Community policing means more than educating the public about the work of the police department, the dangers of drug abuse, or crime prevention. Community-oriented policing means actively engaging the community in defining problems, setting priorities and goals for the police, and finding solutions to community problems.[97] Foot patrol is a central part of this approach.[98] Getting police officers out of their patrol cars and onto the streets to meet the people who live there has proven to be good for crime prevention, good for community peace of mind, and good for police morale.

Community policing has also been called "problem-oriented policing."[99] The theory behind problem-oriented policing is that a few common underlying conditions and problems lead to seemingly distinct police incidents. In order to understand the incidents, police officers must examine their causes in the broadest possible way. Police should go beyond criminal justice methods, like arrest, and explore other avenues.[100]

Problem-oriented policing is proactive, not reactive.[101] With the focus on patrol to prevent crime and "rapid response" to catch criminals, modern police have become increasingly isolated and reactive.[102] Studies show that by the time officers arrive at a crime scene, no matter how quick the response time, it is generally already too late. Many crimes are discovered only when victims return to their cars or homes to find them stolen or broken into. Rapid response may provide some comfort to the victim, but it is often not enough to prevent the crime or to catch the perpetrator. In crimes where the victim is confronted by the perpetrator, rapid response has proven equally insufficient. If the victim/witness waits more than five minutes to call the police, the perpetrator will be gone.[103] In Kansas City, only 2 percent of the police department's serious crime calls were thought to merit a rapid response.[104] This finding is not unique to Kansas City.[105]

Community policing and problem-oriented policing have much in common. Both seek to balance reactive and proactive strategies, responding to crises and emergencies but also responding to what the community wants and needs. Both encourage creativity and flexibility in dealing with complex urban problems. Both prefer specialization and focus over coverage of vast geographic areas. Both favor decentralization of police command.[106] Both seek a police-community partnership.

Community-oriented policing has the potential to change the relationship between the police and the community, and to have some impact on the layered antagonism that spawned the Rodney King incident and the many other examples of violence and degradation testified to in the hearings. Community policing means to defuse the insider/outsider vision of the police, to overcome police resistance to change, to chip away at police culture.[107]

H Some Form of Civilian Review Must Be Adopted by All Police Departments

The NAACP hearings have reaffirmed the increasingly widespread recognition that police misconduct must be taken seriously and that institutional mechanisms must be firmly in place to discipline offending officers promptly and adequately. There is a growing national consensus that some form of strong, independent, civilian oversight is necessary.[108] As Boston's St. Clair Commission concluded, "Only by bringing community members into the [disciplinary] process can [the internal affairs division] hope to regain credibility and restore the public's confidence that the . . . [p]olice can be trusted to investigate themselves."[109]

The Christopher Commission found in a survey of the twenty largest cities in the country (and of Madison, Wisconsin) that thirteen have some form of civilian review: six have wholly *civilian* review, four have boards with a combination of sworn officers and civilians, and three have parallel review processes (police and civilian) operating at the same time.[110] The majority of the cities in which NAACP hearings were held reflected these varieties of civilian review, each having its own unique nomenclature and format.[111]

There was a strong, clear call from civilians (and some police) who testified at the hearings for an independent review board. For most, the need for independence was based on long, painful experience, which had taught them that the police cannot effectively investigate and discipline themselves. As one Los Angeles witness testified, "[T]he remedy is a Civilian Review Board independent of the police department, independent of an out-of-control department that . . . tends to give a green light to those officers [who engage in misconduct]. . . ."[112]

The NAACP recognizes the complexity of the issue of civilian review and that the form of review must vary from municipality to municipality. However, we recommend that the following be a part of every civilian review process:

1 The civilian review board must have independent investigatory power

Independent investigatory power is "absolutely necessary to do[ing] this job."[113] This power should include independent investigative staffs,[114] subpoena power,[115] and the power to compel officers to cooperate.[116]

2 Civilian review boards should be composed of a majority of non–law enforcement personnel

The NAACP strongly recommends that the majority of those who sit on civilian review boards be *civilians*. These boards must be viewed as nonpartisan and independent in order to gain the trust and confidence of the entire community. In particular, civilian review boards must be independent of police authority.[117]

3   Hearings should be open to the public

Public confidence in and access to civilian review boards is imperative. The process should be straightforward and easy to understand. Many witnesses at the hearings testified that too many citizens are unfamiliar with civilian review processes.[118] Several testified that those processes need to be made more visible.[119] A number of witnesses also testified that there is a widespread lack of trust when review boards work "behind closed doors," making public only the "results."[120]

The problem of police conduct and community relations will not be solved overnight. As a result of six public hearings and a collection of other data, the NAACP has identified a number of significant issues and has proposed a number of far-reaching reforms. However, the NAACP recognizes that it has just begun a long-overdue process of change. The NAACP intends to ensure that the issues this report has raised will continue to be addressed well into the next century.

▲ N O T E S ▲

Notes to Introduction

1   *See* N.Y. TIMES, November 8, 1992, at 24.

2   REPORT OF THE INDEPENDENT COMMISSION ON THE LOS ANGELES POLICE DEPARTMENT (1991) [hereinafter CHRISTOPHER COMMISSION REPORT].

3   Poll by Princeton Survey Researching Associates for Lifetime Television (April 1991).

4   Poll by ABC News/Washington Post (October 1989).

5   Poll by Newsweek (February 1988).

6   *Id.*

7   Poll by New York Times/WCBS-TV (January 1988).

8   GALE RESEARCH INSTITUTE, INC., STATISTICAL RECORD OF BLACK AMERICA (1990).

9   Frank Lumpkin, quoted in STUDS TERKEL, RACE 90–91 (1992).

10   Testimony of Lindell Beamon, INDIANAPOLIS HEARINGS, December 17, 1991, at 348, 350–51.

11   *See* MALCOLM K. SPARROW ET AL., BEYOND 911 41–47 (1990).

12   *See id.* at 44 ("[T]he simple fact [is] that the police seem to be failing in their primary mission of crime control. Crime rates remain at historic highs in the United States. Clearance rates, which measure the fraction of reported crime solved . . . remain quite low: currently less than 30 percent of robberies . . . and less than 15 percent of burglaries. The police do not seem to be controlling crime."). *See also* ELLIOT CURRIE, CON-FRONTING CRIME 4–20 (1985).

13   *See* CURRIE, *supra* note 12, at 144–221, 224–78. For a discussion of crime prevention through policing, *see* SPARROW ET AL., *supra* note 11, at 3–7, 44–47; HERMAN GOLDSTEIN, PROBLEM-ORIENTED POLICING 21–26, 32–49 (1990); Mark H. Moore et al., *Crime and Policing,* PERSPECTIVES ON POLICING, no. 2 (National Institute of Justice and Harvard University, 1988); James Q. Wilson & George L. Kelling, *Making Neighborhoods Safe,* ATLANTIC MONTHLY, Feb. 1989, at 46; James Q. Wilson & George L. Kelling, *Broken Windows,* ATLANTIC MONTHLY, March 1982, at 29.

14   LIVING COLOUR, *Which Way to America, on* VIVID (CBS Records 1988). Used by permission of Famous Music Corporation.

15   Salim Muwakkil, before the first Rodney King verdict, quoted in TERKEL, *supra* note 9, at 171.

16   ANDREW HACKER, TWO NATIONS 46 (1992). *See also* Testimony of Jeanette Amadeo, MIAMI HEARINGS, November 13, 1991, at 701 ("I have no . . . [respect for the police]. If something was happening to me, I wouldn't want the police officer to be called.").

17   HACKER, *supra* note 16, at 180. *See also* CHRISTOPHER JENCKS, RE-THINKING SOCIAL POLICY 98 (1992) ("... [B]lacks currently account for about half of all arrests for rape and murder and two thirds of all arrests for robbery in the United States, even though they constitute less than one eighth of the population. . . . The conclusion that blacks are five to ten times more likely than whites to commit most violent crimes is almost inescapable.").

18   HACKER, *supra* note 16, at 180.

19   *See* C. Black, *America's Lost Generation,* BOSTON GLOBE, Mar. 4, 1990, at 69.

20   HACKER, *supra* note 16, at 180. The term "violation" refers to either a probation or parole violation, the commission of which often means a sentence of incarceration.

21   *See* Charles J. Ogletree, *Does Race Matter in Criminal Prosecutions?,* CHAMPION, July 1991, at 10–12. *See also* Lee P. Brown, *Bridges over Troubled Water: A Perspective on Policing in the Black Community, in* BLACK PERSPECTIVES ON CRIME AND THE CRIMINAL JUSTICE SYSTEM (Robert L. Woodson, ed., 1977); R. L. McNeely & C. Pope, *Race, Crime, and Criminal Justice: An Overview, in* 2 RACE, CRIME, AND CRIMINAL JUSTICE 13–14 (R. L. McNeely & C. Pope, eds., 1981).

22   392 U.S. 1 (1968).

23   MICHAEL BROWN, WORKING THE STREET: POLICE DISCRETION AND THE DILEMMAS OF REFORM 166 (1981). *See also Developments in the Law—Race and the Criminal Process,* 101 HARVARD L. REV. 1472 (1988); SHERI LYNN JOHNSON, *Race and the Decision to Detain a Suspect,* 93 YALE L.J. 214 (1983).

24   Richard Delgado, *"Rotten Social Background": Should the Criminal Law Recognize a Defense of Severe Environmental Deprivation?,* 3 LAW AND INEQ. 9, 30 (1985); *see also Police in N.Y. are Cited for Racial Hostility,* PHILADELPHIA INQUIRER, Nov. 15, 1984, at 4A, col. 1 (House subcommittee investigation found that police commented on and arrested blacks for behavior they would overlook in whites).

25   FLORIDA ADVISORY COMMITTEE TO THE UNITED STATES COMMISSION ON CIVIL RIGHTS, POLICE-COMMUNITY RELATIONS IN MIAMI 3 (1989), MIAMI HEARINGS, November 12–13, 1991.

26   James Fyfe, *Race and Extreme Police-Citizen Violence, in* 2 RACE, CRIME, AND CRIMINAL JUSTICE 92 (R. L. McNeely & C. Pope, eds., 1981).

27   HACKER, *supra* note 16, at 189.

28   *Id.*

29   *Id.* at 187–88.

30   *See* ALEX KOTLOWITZ, THERE ARE NO CHILDREN HERE (1990).

31   BRUCE WRIGHT, BLACK ROBES, WHITE JUSTICE (1987).

32   WILSON GRIER & PRICE COBBS, BLACK RAGE 149 (1968).

33   *See* CURRIE, *supra* note 12, at 146–51. Though most poor people of all races labor honestly, sometimes for the lowest of wages, there is a wealth of evidence linking crime with social and economic inequality. *Id.*

at 146. *See also* JENCKS, *supra* note 17, at 114–16 (asserting that "relative deprivation" is a better explanation for crime than is poverty).

34   REPORT OF THE NATIONAL ADVISORY COMMISSION ON CIVIL DISORDERS, 6, 10 (1968).

35   *Id.*

36   HACKER, *supra* note 16, at 99.

37   JAMES GARBARINO ET AL., NO PLACE TO BE A CHILD 149 (1991).

38   *See* HACKER, *supra* note 16, at 100 ("Of course, there is a white underclass. Its members can be found among the addicted and the homeless, among men who have never held steady jobs, and women who have spent many years on welfare. The nation's prisons still have plenty of white criminals, some of whom are quite vicious and others who have made careers in small-time larcenies. Even so, neither sociologists nor journalists have shown much interest in depicting poor whites as a 'class.' In large measure, the reason is racial. For whites, poverty tends to be viewed as atypical or accidental. Among blacks, it comes close to being seen as a natural outgrowth of their history and culture. At times, it almost appears as if white poverty must be covered up, lest it blemish the reputation of the dominant race.").

39   *Id.* at 46.

40   *See* Marc Cooper, *Dum Da Dum-Dum: L.A. Beware: The Mother of All Police Departments Is Here to Serve and Protect*, VILLAGE VOICE, April 16, 1991, at 26.

41   *Id.*

42   *See* SIDNEY L. HARRING, POLICING A CLASS SOCIETY: THE EXPERIENCE OF AMERICAN CITIES, 1865–1915 6–7 (1983). While Harring's analysis of policing focuses on class rather than on race, many of his observations ring true for both.

43   *See* MARTHA MINOW, MAKING ALL THE DIFFERENCE 3 (1990) ("When we identify one thing as unlike the others, we are dividing the world; we use our language to exclude, to distinguish—to discriminate. This last word may be the one that most recognizably raises the issues about which I worry. Sometimes, classifications express and implement prejudice, racism, sexism, anti-Semitism, intolerance for difference. Of course, there are 'real differences' in the world; each person differs in countless ways from each other person. But when we simplify and sort, we focus on some traits rather than others, and we assign consequences to the presence and absence of the traits we make significant."). *Cf.* Cooper, *supra* note 40 ([conversation with three white members of the Los Angeles Police Department] " 'Life down there is very cheap. People are dying there while we are sitting here talking. . . . It's really us against them. . . . [T]here is a lot of crime down there. You look at the guy on the corner and you know he's not working, he's waiting to rip off a purse. You got the dope dealers there in their nice cars. . . . The people committing the crimes hate us. And the good people don't understand us either. . . . [The] problem down

there is no family structure. You see children having children with no fucking idea who the father is. In the black communities all the kids have different last names. All the mothers have six, eight kids and no fucking idea where they are. And they couldn't give a damn because they are too busy pumping out another kid. Picking up the government check. Every Cadillac and Mercedes you stop in the south end of town has food stamps in the glove box.' "). *See also* Bill Clinton's acceptance speech at the 1992 Democratic National Convention ("There is no them, there is only us.").

44   *See, e.g.,* SPARROW ET AL., *supra* note 11, at 50–54; CONNIE FLETCHER, PURE COP (1991); CONNIE FLETCHER, WHAT COPS KNOW (1990); EGON BITTNER, THE FUNCTIONS OF THE POLICE IN MODERN SOCIETY (1980); JONATHAN RUBENSTEIN, CITY POLICE (1973); ARTHUR NIEDERHOFFER, BEHIND THE SHIELD (1969). *But see* EDWIN J. DELATTRE, CHARACTER AND COPS (1989) (describing an alternative culture for policing).

45   *See* SPARROW ET AL., *supra* note 11, at 50–54 ("These are the beliefs that, for better or worse, now play a large part in fashioning police conduct. They reflect the values that are drummed into new recruits informally as soon as they have left the academy; they reflect the values that are perpetually reinforced among peers in locker rooms and cafeterias."). *See also* Myron W. Orfield, Jr., *Deterrence, Perjury, and the Heater Factor: An Exclusionary Rule in the Chicago Criminal Courts,* 63 U. COLO. L. REV. 75 (1992) (examining the effect of the exclusionary rule on police practice in Chicago).

46   Testimony of Migdaly Rivas, MIAMI HEARINGS, November 13, 1991, at 634.

47   *See id.* at 634–35.

48   *See* SPARROW ET AL., *supra* note 11, at 51–54.

Notes to Findings

1   Many examples of racially motivated police sweeps come to mind, too many to list. Several fairly recent episodes illustrate the problem. In 1992, Minneapolis police were stopping and searching almost all black men in the course of a hunt for two black men who allegedly killed a police officer. *See* WASHINGTON POST, October 21, 1992, at A3. The police investigation of the Carol Stuart murder in Boston in 1989, in which an African American man was falsely accused of the killing by the actual murderer, Charles Stuart, began with a massive sweep of the Mission Hill area of Boston, an African American neighborhood. In 1985, Philadelphia police began their investigation of a highly publicized police killing by sweeping through Spring Garden, a Hispanic area. In the course of the sweep, Hispanic people, old and young, male and female, light and dark, were stopped and questioned; some were even subpoenaed to the district attorney's office for questioning. *See Spring Garden United Neighbors v.*

City of Philadelphia, 614 F. Supp. 1350 (E.D. Pa. 1985). Several years later, the Philadelphia police had apparently not learned their lesson. In Operation Center City Stalker, the police, based on a very general composite of a black man who had been assaulting women at knife-point in the late afternoon in Center City, were stopping every African American man in a several-mile radius. *See* Charles J. Ogletree, *Does Race Matter in Criminal Prosecutions?,* CHAMPION, July 1991, at 7, 10–12; Nat Hentoff, *Forgetting the Fourth Amendment in Philadelphia,* WASHINGTON POST, April 16, 1988, at A25.

2   One example was the "search on sight" campaign by the Boston Police Department in their strategy to combat drugs. As part of the 1988 operation, officers routinely stopped black youths they suspected of being in gangs or of being "up to no good." *See* Ogletree, *supra* note 1, at 11–12.

3   The above "search on sight" operation included taking black youths off buses and making them pull down their pants in public for body searches.

4   *See* Ogletree, *supra* note 1, at 12.

5   Testimony of Bernard T. Holmes, legal counsel, Virginia Beach NAACP, NORFOLK HEARINGS, November 6, 1991, at 63–65.

6   *See* Testimony of Andrew Cherry, Barry University, MIAMI HEARINGS, November 13, 1991, at 587 (testifying that 35% of the homeless population was white and 42% was black in November 1988, whereas 13% was white and 67% was black as of May 1991).

7   *Id.* at 589.

8   *Id.* at 587–89.

9   *Id.* at 588.

10   *Id.* at 589–90.

11   *See* Testimony of John Makemson, vice-chair, Miami Branch, ACLU, MIAMI HEARINGS, November 12, 1991, at 141–42.

12   *See* Testimony of Andrew Cherry, MIAMI HEARINGS, November 13, 1991, at 592.

13   Sheri Lynn Johnson, *Race and the Decision to Detain a Suspect,* 93 YALE L.J. 214, 236 (1983).

14   The Fourth Amendment of the United States Constitution prohibits the search and seizure of a person without probable cause.

15   392 U.S. 1 (1968).

16   *Id.* at 15.

17   Testimony of Ernie Neal, vice-president, Miami Chapter of NOBLE (National Organization of Black Law Enforcement Executives), MIAMI HEARINGS, November 13, 1991, at 580–81. *See also* Testimony of Norma Jean Stokes, INDIANAPOLIS HEARINGS, December 17, 1991, at 378–82 (describing armed stop and search of two African American women and a teenage boy in the course of a police hunt for two black men).

18   An example is the call by many mothers in black communities

for metal detectors and random locker searches in public high schools to combat the flow of weapons into the schools.

19   *See, e.g.,* Lee P. Brown, *Bridges over Troubled Water: A Perspective on Policing in the Black Community, in* BLACK PERSPECTIVES ON CRIME AND THE CRIMINAL JUSTICE SYSTEM (Robert L. Woodson, ed., 1977), at 79; R. L. McNeely & C. Pope, *Race, Crime, and Criminal Justice: An Overview, in* 2 RACE, CRIME, AND CRIMINAL JUSTICE 13–14 (R. L. McNeely & C. Pope, eds., 1981); James Fyfe, *Blind Justice: Police Shootings in Memphis,* 73 JOURNAL OF CRIMINAL LAW AND CRIMINOLOGY 707, 718–20 (1982); Johnson, *supra* note 13.

20   *See* Marc Mauer, *Young Black Men and the Criminal Justice System: A Growing National Problem,* SENTENCING PROJECT, February 1990.

21   *See* Testimony of Ray Fauntroy, president of the Miami Chapter of the Southern Christian Leadership Conference, MIAMI HEARINGS, November 13, 1991, at 705.

22   This has been the collective experience of the staff of the Criminal Justice Institute in their representation of clients charged with criminal offenses in Roxbury, Dorchester, and Cambridge, Massachusetts.

23   Testimony of Joseph Johnson, INDIANAPOLIS HEARINGS, December 17, 1991, at 401.

24   *Id.* at 401, 407.

25   *Id.* at 402.

26   *Id.* at 402–3.

27   *Id.* at 403.

28   *Id.* at 404–6. When he appeared in court after a night in jail, the judge told him "how tough he was, and that he [had] locked up a lot of blacks when he was a military judge in the Army." *Id.* at 405. *See also* MICHAEL E. DYSON, REFLECTING BLACK 191–93 (1993) (African American professor recounts an incident involving a bank error, during which the bank manager threatened to call the police if he did not leave).

29   Testimony of Mary Redd, Urban League, NORFOLK HEARINGS, November 6, 1991, at 147. *See also* Testimony of Rev. Willie Simms, Black Affairs Program, Metro-Dade Department of Community Affairs, MIAMI HEARINGS, November 12, 1991, at 67 ("[W]e need to deal with that simplistic approach. . . . If you think that every African American male is a criminal then you can't help but approach them in that style.").

30   "ABC News Nightline" (ABC Television broadcast, September 2, 1992).

31   *See also* Ogletree, *supra* note 1, at 7, 12–13 ("Although African Americans comprise twelve percent of the national population, they account for almost fifty percent of the prison population. . . . One out of every four black men between the ages of 20–29 is under the control of the criminal justice system, in prison, on probation, or on parole."); Marc Mauer, *Americans Behind Bars: A Comparison of International Rates of Incarceration,* SENTENCING PROJECT, January 1989; Mauer, *supra* note 20.

32   "ABC News Nightline" (ABC Television broadcast, September 2, 1992). *See also* Testimony of Dr. Larry Capp, psychologist, MIAMI HEARINGS, November 12, 1991, at 228–29 ("I think that perception [that black citizens are more apt to be the victims of police misconduct than white citizens] is true and I think particularly with respect to black males of all ages and especially with respect to black teenagers. . . . I think it exist[s] as a result of several incidents that have occurred here in the South Florida area involving black males who have been hurt, injured or killed at the hands of law enforcement officials here.").

33   *See* Testimony of George E. Mins, president, Virginia Beach NAACP, NORFOLK HEARINGS, November 6, 1991, at 184.

34   *See* Testimony of Ernie Neal, vice-president, Miami Chapter of NOBLE, MIAMI HEARINGS, November 13, 1991, at 581 ("In making these decisions [whether to invoke the process of the criminal law], police [officers] rely on such visible attributes of status, as attitude, color, age, dress or demeanor, as well as the nature of the offense itself. . . .").

35   *See* Testimony of Bernard T. Holmes, legal counsel, Virginia Beach NAACP, NORFOLK HEARINGS, November 6, 1991, at 63. *See also* Testimony of Dr. Willie Williams, Fair Share Job Committee of PULSE (People United to Lead the Struggle for Equality), MIAMI HEARINGS, November 13, 1991, at 510–11 ("[W]e have found out . . . that a lot of times when police stop blacks, young blacks, the ones in the street, they like to intimidate them. They like to call them out . . . cuss them, and one of the main things that they call them, to try and get them riled up, is 'boy.' I think you know how that infuriates young blacks. I think you know how they feel about being called 'boy' by a white person. Once they become intimidated and riled up or raise their hands, then this is enough . . . for a police [officer] to say he is resisting arrest. . . .").

36   "20/20" (ABC Television broadcast, November 6, 1992).

37   *Id. See also* Testimony of Rev. Willie Simms, Black Affairs Program, Metro-Dade Department of Community Affairs, MIAMI HEARINGS, November 12, 1991, at 67 ("If you think that everybody that drives a fancy car is involved in crime then my daughter and my son cannot drive my vehicle to the store.").

38   "ABC News Nightline" (ABC Television broadcast, September 2, 1992).

39   *Id.*

40   Testimony of Mary Redd, Urban League, NORFOLK HEARINGS, November 6, 1991, at 147–50.

41   *See* Testimony of Glenn Stewart, MIAMI HEARINGS, November 13, 1991, at 684–85, 692.

42   Testimony of Chief Paul Anee, Indianapolis Police Department (1986–91), INDIANAPOLIS HEARINGS, December 17, 1991, at 48–49.

43   *See* Testimony of Maj. Sheldon Darden, chief of operations, Norfolk Police Department, NORFOLK HEARINGS, November 6, 1991, at 59.

44   *See* Testimony of Rev. Joseph Green, Norfolk Hearings, November 6, 1991, at 29–30.

45   Testimony of Chief Michael McCrary, Signal Hill Police Department, Los Angeles County, Los Angeles Hearings, December 4, 1991, at 126–27.

46   *See* Florida Advisory Committee to the United States Commission on Civil Rights, Police-Community Relations in Miami. "According to most of the community leaders [present at the forum], the incidents which led to the riots of 1980, 1982, and 1989 [in Miami] show a common pattern of abuse, disrespect, insensitivity, poor police practices and outright errors on the part of the affected police officers. Time and again, said the leaders, this has led to loss of lives, property, and respect from the black community for police departments all too often seen as the invading enemy." *Id.* at 16.

Maintaining independent records on police-action shootings becomes increasingly important as the political pressure to control such statistics unfolds. In the above case, it is unclear whether any of the shootings between 1979 and 1988 as reported to the Florida Advisory Committee are included in the seventeen shootings that the state's attorney's office listed as "questionable." It is in the interest of the police departments for the incidence of police misconduct to be as low as possible. Official statistics underestimate actual police misconduct, partly because the incidence of police abuse and police misconduct is underreported and partly because there are very few independent agencies with access to this information in its raw form.

47   *See* written submission by Dr. Willie Williams, Fair Share Job Committee of PULSE, Miami Hearings, November 13, 1991.

48   *See* Testimony of Dr. Willie Williams, Fair Share Job Committee of PULSE, Miami Hearings, November 13, 1991, at 492 (testifying the police reported McFadden died from a drug overdose, yet there were visible marks all over his body that appeared to indicate that he was severely beaten).

49   *See* Testimony of David Honig, general counsel, Miami-Dade Branch, NAACP, Miami Hearings, November 12, 1991, at 174–75, and written submission to hearings, *Summary of Documented Complaints of Police Misconduct Received by the Miami-Dade Branch of the NAACP*, January 1990–August 1991.

50   Testimony of David Honig, general counsel, Miami-Dade Branch, NAACP, Miami Hearings, November 12, 1991, at 172.

51   *See* written submission from David Honig, general counsel, Miami-Dade Branch, NAACP, *Summary of Documented Complaints of Police Misconduct Received by the Miami-Dade Branch of the NAACP*, January 1990–August 1991, Miami Hearings, November 12, 1991.

52   Testimony of Johnnie L. Cochran, attorney, LOS ANGELES HEAR-INGS, December 3, 1991, at 65–66.

53   *See* Testimony of Henry Paxton, attorney for the Henry Peco Justice Committee, LOS ANGELES HEARINGS, December 3, 1991, at 163.

54   *See id.*

55   *See* Testimony of Ada Edwards, chairperson, Ida Delaney/Byron Gillum Justice Committee, HOUSTON HEARINGS, November 19, 1991, at 362; Testimony of Scott Sanes, attorney, HOUSTON HEARINGS, November 19, 1991, at 408. *See also New Turmoil over Police in Houston,* N.Y. TIMES, Dec. 10, 1989, at 36; *Rift Remains a Year after Delaney Slain,* HOUSTON CHRONI-CLE, Oct. 28, 1990, at 1C; *Officer Intoxicated,* HOUSTON POST, November 4, 1989, at A1.

56   *See* Testimony of Donald W. Cook, attorney, LOS ANGELES HEAR-INGS, December 3, 1991, at 47–48.

57   *Id.*

58   *Id.* at 48.

59   *Id.* at 50–53. Cook testified that LAPD use-of-force statistics show how often officers "have to resort to some type of physical force of a significant type." These statistics are distinct from dog-bite statistics. *Id.* at 53.

60   *Id.* at 54–58.

61   SEATTLE TIMES, July 14, 1992, at D1.

62   LOS ANGELES TIMES, Jan. 27, 1989, at 2.

63   LOS ANGELES TIMES, Dec. 12, 1991, at Metro, p. 1. To underscore the need for reform in this area, the LOS ANGELES TIMES, October 14, 1992, at Metro, p. 2, reported that the Los Angeles Police Commission recently acknowledged a new direction in the use of police dogs when it announced in October 1992 that it now recommends that the canine unit be retrained to use the "bark and alert" method of finding alleged suspects first. The recommendation was made after the American Civil Liberties Union threatened a class-action suit based on the use of police dogs.

64   Testimony of Selvei Burris, INDIANAPOLIS HEARINGS, December 17, 1991, at 312–17.

65   *Id.* at 312–15.

66   Mr. Burris testified: "[T]he only thing I can think of was it had to be a racial issue. The four policemen were white, the young lady was white. And there was no other reason for it." *Id.* at 316.

67   Testimony of Judy Steen Davis, MIAMI HEARINGS, November 13, 1991, at 558–68.

68   Testimony of Jody Lee, INDIANAPOLIS HEARINGS, December 18, 1991, at 531–32, 543.

69   *Id.* at 541.

70   *See* Testimony of Mr. and Mrs. Willie Mitchell and Testimony of Dorothy Johnson, MIAMI HEARINGS, November 13, 1991, at 534–58. Johnson, a neighbor, testified that she saw the incident: "The emotions that

welled up in me when I witnessed the attack of [the Mitchell] family made me realize just how helpless we are against the police and political power structure." Testimony of Dorothy Johnson, MIAMI HEARINGS, November 13, 1991, at 536–37.

71   *See, e.g.,* Testimony of citizens, INDIANAPOLIS HEARINGS, December 17, 1991, at 312–532.

72   *See, e.g.,* Testimony of Carl Kelley, INDIANAPOLIS HEARINGS, December 17, 1991, at 358–59.

73   *See* Testimony of James Foster, LOS ANGELES HEARINGS, December 3, 1991, at 44–45.

74   *Id.*

75   *Id.* at 45, 79.

76   Testimony of David L. Perkins, MIAMI HEARINGS, November 13, 1991, at 670–71.

77   Testimony of Alexander Kelly, MIAMI HEARINGS, November 13, 1991, at 680–81.

78   *See* Testimony of George E. Mins, president, Virginia Beach NAACP, NORFOLK HEARINGS, November 6, 1991, at 5. *See also* Testimony of Cynthia McMurrey, attorney, HOUSTON HEARINGS, November 19, 1991, at 176 (testifying that whenever she sees people with cuts, scrapes, or abrasions, they are always charged with resisting arrest); Testimony of Dr. Willie Williams, MIAMI HEARINGS, November 13, 1991, at 498; Testimony of Kathleen Worthy, Community-Police Relations Committee of UP-PAC (Unrepresented People, Positive Action Council), MIAMI HEARINGS, November 13, 1991, at 479–80 ("Another common occurrence is the practice of throwing the book at young black men where police officers expect a brutality complaint. . . . They beat up the young people, then charge them with an assortment of crimes. . . . Most times the young people simply plead guilty, under pressure, and take a short sentence or probation instead of going to trial.").

79   *See* Testimony of William P. Robinson, member of the Virginia House of Delegates, NORFOLK HEARINGS, November 6, 1991, at 126.

80   *See id.* at 127–28. *See also* Testimony of Joyce Armstrong, ACLU, ST. LOUIS HEARINGS, December 6, 1991, at 58–60 (Twenty-two percent of persons who wrote to the ACLU about police misconduct alleged injury at the hands of the police, either during the arrest or while in custody; 19 percent of the complaints involved persons who required medical attention as a result of police abuse. "These individuals often end up facing charges such as resisting arrest or interfering with the officer, destruction of public property or assaulting an officer."). *Id.* at 59.

81   *See, e.g.,* Testimony of David Shaheed, president-elect, Marion County Bar Association, INDIANAPOLIS HEARINGS, December 17, 1991, at 136–37 (testifying that it is routine practice for defendants to be asked to sign an agreement not to sue the police, in exchange for the dismissal of criminal charges: "It's something that's on the computer, and it's just

a matter of printing out the form, changing the names, and having the defendant . . . sign the release.").

82   Testimony of Verner Lee Shepard, LOS ANGELES HEARINGS, December 3, 1991, at 133.

83   *See* Testimony of Chief Elizabeth Watson, Houston Police Department, HOUSTON HEARINGS, November 19, 1991, at 52; Testimony of Fred Taylor, director, Metro-Dade Police Department, MIAMI HEARINGS, November 12, 1991, at 105; Testimony of Chief Calvin Ross, Miami Police Department, MIAMI HEARINGS, November 13, 1991, at 447–48; Testimony of Chief Ian Shipley, Chesapeake Police Department, NORFOLK HEARINGS, November 6, 1991, at 80; Testimony of Chief Charles Wall, Virginia Beach Police Department, NORFOLK HEARINGS, November 6, 1991, at 80.

84   None of these departments provided sufficient data to determine whether the use of deadly force has decreased since adoption of a more restrictive policy.

85   *See* Testimony of Chief Calvin Ross, Miami Police Department, MIAMI HEARINGS, November 13, 1991, at 448–49.

86   *See* Testimony of Mayor William Hudnut, INDIANAPOLIS HEARINGS, December 17, 1991, at 13.

87   *See* Testimony of Chief Ian Shipley, Chesapeake Police Department, NORFOLK HEARINGS, November 6, 1991, at 40–42.

88   *See* Testimony of Chief Lawrence L. Binkley, Long Beach Police Department, LOS ANGELES HEARINGS, December 4, 1991, at 65.

89   *See* Testimony of William P. Robinson, member of the Virginia House of Delegates, NORFOLK HEARINGS, November 6, 1991, at 119; Testimony of Joyce Armstrong, ACLU, ST. LOUIS HEARINGS, December 6, 1991, at 63 (testifying that the ACLU does not hear that the whole police department is bad, but there is a percentage of officers who are regularly involved in police misuse of force).

90   *See* Testimony of William P. Robinson, member of the Virginia House of Delegates, NORFOLK HEARINGS, November 6, 1991, at 119, 134–35.

91   *Id.* at 129 (testifying that there are no procedures in place that result in a full hearing and possible disciplinary action in cases of alleged misconduct where there are no independent witnesses).

92   *See* Testimony of Mary Redd, Urban League, NORFOLK HEARINGS, November 6, 1991, at 151–52.

93   *See, e.g.,* Testimony of Kathleen Worthy, UP-PAC, MIAMI HEARINGS, November 13, 1991, at 485.

94   REPORT OF THE INDEPENDENT COMMISSION ON THE LOS ANGELES POLICE DEPARTMENT (1991) [hereinafter CHRISTOPHER COMMISSION REPORT], at 37–38 (referring to a June 1991 news series in the LOS ANGELES DAILY NEWS).

95   *Id.* at 39.

96   *Id.* at 37–38.

97   *Id.* at 32.

98   *Wave of Abuse Claims Laid to a Few Officers,* BOSTON GLOBE, Oct. 4, 1992, at 1, 28.

99   *Id.*

100   Report of the Boston Police Department Management Review Commission (1992) [hereinafter St. Clair Commission Report], at 112.

101   *Id.* at 110.

102   *Id.* at 112.

103   *Id.* at 112. The thirteen officers had "generated an incredible total of 246 prior complaints." *Id.*

104   The Christopher Commission found that three of the four officers indicted by state authorities in the Rodney King beating had been the subject of prior excessive-force complaints. One had been suspended in 1987 for kicking and hitting a Latino suspect with a baton and was also named in a 1985 excessive-force complaint that was "not sustained" by the LAPD. Another officer was accused of using excessive force against a handcuffed suspect in 1986, which was held "not sustained" by the LAPD; the same officer has been sued for breaking a citizen's arm with a baton. A third officer was suspended for not reporting his use of force against a suspect after a pursuit; the complaint was "not sustained." Christopher Commission Report, at 12.

105   *See* Testimony of Scott Sanes, attorney, Houston Hearings, November 19, 1991, at 400–409, 412–13.

106   *See* Testimony of Assistant Chief Jimmy L. Dotson, Houston Police Department, Houston Hearings, November 19, 1991, at 131–35 (also testified that the case was no-billed by a grand jury and that the officer was subsequently fired).

107   *See* Testimony of Fred Taylor, director, Metro-Dade Police Department, Miami Hearings, November 12, 1991, at 86, 114.

108   The annual report identifies officers complained against in two or more quarters, as well as those having four or more complaints, seven or more use-of-force reports, or two or more shootings in twelve months. *See* written materials submitted by Metro-Dade Police Department, Miami Hearings, November 12–13, 1991.

109   *See* Testimony of Fred Taylor, director, Metro-Dade Police Department, Miami Hearings, November 12, 1991, at 86, and written materials submitted by Metro-Dade Police Department, "Professional Compliance Bureau Early Identification System," Section 6, Miami Hearings, November 12–13, 1991. The number of officers identified in the quarterly reports was 56 in 1982, 19 in 1983, 14 in 1984, 37 in 1985, 31 in 1986, 17 in 1987, 27 in 1988, 60 in 1989, 47 in 1990, and 19 in the first half of 1991.

110   *See* Testimony of Dr. Larry Capp, psychologist, Miami Hearings, November 12, 1991, at 211; Testimony of Chief Calvin Ross, Miami Police Department, Miami Hearings, November 13, 1991, at 449–50.

111   *See* Testimony of Dr. Larry Capp, psychologist, Miami Hearings, November 12, 1991, at 230–33 (testifying that the recommendations for

treatment are followed by the department, but not necessarily by the officers, and that he monitors the recommendations because his firm would generally be involved in the treatment).

112   *See* Testimony of Chief Elizabeth Watson, Houston Police Department, HOUSTON HEARINGS, November 19, 1991, at 8.

113   *See* Testimony of Assistant Chief Jimmy L. Dotson, Houston Police Department, HOUSTON HEARINGS, November 19, 1991, at 102, 103–4 ("[I]f you can change behavior, you can change attitudes. . . .").

114   *Id.* at 103–4.

115   *See* Testimony of Chief Elizabeth Watson, Houston Police Department, HOUSTON HEARINGS, November 19, 1991, at 8.

116   *See* Testimony of Chief Lawrence L. Binkley, Long Beach Police Department, LOS ANGELES HEARINGS, December 4, 1991, at 65.

117   *Id.* at 66.

118   *Id.* at 67 (testifying that the audits revealed some racial slurs and misconduct, for which discipline was initiated).

119   *See* Testimony of Maj. Dennis R. Long, St. Louis County Police Department, ST. LOUIS HEARINGS, December 6, 1991, at 12 (There was no testimony as to how internal affairs identified patterns of abuse, the numbers of officers so identified, or the actions taken by internal affairs regarding those officers.).

120   *See* Testimony of Chief Clarence Harmon, St. Louis Metropolitan Police Department, ST. LOUIS HEARINGS, December 6, 1991, at 53.

121   *See* Testimony of Maj. Sheldon Darden, chief of operations, Norfolk Police Department, NORFOLK HEARINGS, November 6, 1991, at 61.

122   *Id.* at 91–92.

123   *See* Testimony of Chief Ian Shipley, Chesapeake Police Department, NORFOLK HEARINGS, November 6, 1991, at 84.

124   *See* Testimony of Chief Charles Wall, Virginia Beach Police Department, NORFOLK HEARINGS, November 6, 1991, at 85.

125   *See* Testimony of Dr. Larry Capp, psychologist, MIAMI HEARINGS, November 12, 1991, at 207–8.

126   *Id.* at 237–38.

127   *See* Testimony of Dr. Ken O'Korie, secretary of the board of directors, Nigerian Foundation, HOUSTON HEARINGS, November 19, 1991, at 351–57 (described the fatal shooting of a Nigerian man by an officer who was then suspended by the chief, reinstated by an arbitrator, and no-billed by a grand jury); Testimony of Ada Edwards, chairperson, Ida Delaney/Byron Gillum Justice Committee, at 359–61 (testifying that 60% of all disciplinary actions taken against Houston officers, by the city or the chief, have been overturned by the arbitration system).

128   *See* Testimony of Mayor Kathryn Whitmire, HOUSTON HEARINGS, November 19, 1991, at 20.

129   *See* Testimony of Sam Jones, Urban League, INDIANAPOLIS HEARINGS, December 17, 1991, at 174, and Testimony of Mayor William Hud-

nut, INDIANAPOLIS HEARINGS, December 17, 1991, at 20. Hudnut testified the Fraternal Order of Police also protects officers from disciplinary action. *Id.*

130   *See* Testimony of Chief Charles Wall, Virginia Beach Police Department, NORFOLK HEARINGS, November 6, 1991, at 66.

131   *See, e.g.,* Testimony of Rev. Rodney Dean, NAACP, ST. LOUIS HEARINGS, December 6, 1991, at 77; Testimony of James Beauford, Urban League, Metropolitan St. Louis, ST. LOUIS HEARINGS, December 6, 1991, at 45; Testimony of Ernest Fields, ST. LOUIS HEARINGS, December 6, 1991, at 92 (Fields, an uninvolved witness to the beating of a young black man, described the young man's fear: "We talked with the guy. The guy himself was afraid to go in and file a complaint.").

132   *See, e.g.,* Testimony of Mary Redd, Urban League, NORFOLK HEARINGS, November 6, 1991, at 7; Testimony of George E. Mins, president, Virginia Beach NAACP, NORFOLK HEARINGS, November 6, 1991, at 7; Testimony of May Walker, African-American Police Officers League, HOUSTON HEARINGS, November 20, 1991, at 100 (brutality complaints come from all types of people, but minorities are less likely to report them); Testimony of James Beauford, Urban League, Metropolitan St. Louis, ST. LOUIS HEARINGS, December 6, 1991, at 36 ("We find that formal complaints are low. But verbal or informal complaints are higher than [they] should be."); Testimony of Dorothy Johnson, MIAMI HEARINGS, November 13, 1991, at 535 ("[M]any of the individuals complain to each other but very few make formal complaints.").

133   *See, e.g.,* Testimony of James Beauford, Urban League, Metropolitan St. Louis, ST. LOUIS HEARINGS, December 6, 1991, at 45 ("I think . . . [the average African American or minority citizen doesn't] know how to [file a complaint] and I think they are afraid to."); Testimony of Johnny Mata, League of United Latin American Citizens, HOUSTON HEARINGS, November 19, 1991, at 181 ("[I]f someone has filed a complaint, then there [are] additional charges filed on those individuals . . . there's also that intimidation, that if you file a complaint, you're going to pay the price. And even [to] the extent that some of these people, when they hit the street again, they're going to be in trouble.").

134   *See, e.g.,* Testimony of Wanda Gonzalez, MIAMI HEARINGS, November 12, 1991, at 302–3 ("[T]hey [are] scared because the thing is they are threatening them if they come over here or if they go to internal affairs, they [are] going to be busted and that is what they have been doing.").

135   Testimony of Rev. James P. Smith, INDIANAPOLIS HEARINGS, December 18, 1991, at 514. (Reverend Smith testified that he had gone to pick up his daughter and her friends from a teenage club and found twenty to thirty sheriff's department units on the premises. As he waited for his daughter, police approached him and told him to leave. When he explained why he was there, an officer told him if he did not leave they

would physically remove him. Other officers came behind him to enforce the order to leave.) *Id.* at 490–94, 508–14.

136   *See, e.g.,* Testimony of James Beauford, Urban League, Metropolitan St. Louis, ST. LOUIS HEARINGS, December 6, 1991, at 36, 45; Testimony of Helen Gros, executive director, Texas ACLU, HOUSTON HEARINGS, November 19, 1991, at 158 ("It takes a tremendous force of will, and an ability to overcome fear, for the average citizen to confront members of the police force, on their own turf, the Internal Affairs Department."); Testimony of Johnny Mata, League of United Latin American Citizens, HOUSTON HEARINGS, November 19, 1991, at 180; Testimony of William P. Robinson, member of the Virginia House of Delegates, NORFOLK HEARINGS, November 6, 1991, at 122 (There is a perception in the community that ". . . even if you complain, nothing's going to happen.").

137   Testimony of Sylvia Brooks, president, Houston Urban League, HOUSTON HEARINGS, November 19, 1991, at 177 ("When they are told that what they must do now is write a letter, is make a personal appearance to the Internal Affairs Department, only a small percentage of the . . . people that I speak with on the telephone, can even envision that as a possibility, and . . . I am sure that they consider their phone call to my office disheartening, discouraging, and what would appear to be to set insurmountable barriers for them being able to take their complaint any further than that telephone call."); Testimony of Helen Gros, executive director, Texas ACLU, November 19, 1991, at 197.

138   Testimony of Ernest Fields, Sr., ST. LOUIS HEARINGS, December 6, 1991, at 93.

139   *See, e.g.,* Testimony of Mary May Dixon, HOUSTON HEARINGS, November 20, 1991, at 367–81, 420 (Ms. Dixon, a Houston woman whose son was shot by police while allegedly driving a stolen car, described insensitive and rude treatment by the police, and said she had no confidence that Houston's internal affairs division (IAD) would give her complaint serious consideration.); Testimony of Michael Gensen, HOUSTON HEARINGS, November 19, 1991, at 422; Testimony of Deborah Gordon, MIAMI HEARINGS, November 13, 1991, at 699 (Ms. Gordon, an African American woman whose son had been shot and killed by the police, was asked if she felt there was anywhere she could go to express concern about her son's mistreatment; she replied: "[T]hat's why I'm glad I had an opportunity to be here to say because I don't know who to go to, who I could go to. Can't go to any of the officers. Can't go to them. They will believe him before they believe me. You know that's just another nigger."); Testimony of Judy Steen Davis, at 565 (testifying that she would advise anyone against going to internal affairs, as it only serves to "perpetuate the police officer's agenda").

140   Testimony of Rev. Bobby Dean, president, Poplar Bluff, Missouri, Branch, NAACP, ST. LOUIS HEARINGS, December 6, 1991, at 72.

141   *See, e.g.,* Testimony of Chief Clarence Harmon, St. Louis Metro-

politan Police Department, St. Louis Hearings, December 6, 1991, at 49 ("I see . . . [the complaint process] working fairly well. I'm not satisfied that it has the broadest reception, particularly in the African American community and as to their belief that they can receive adequate redress or involvement in the process."); Testimony of Chief Elizabeth Watson, Houston Police Department, Houston Hearings, November 19, 1991, at 24 (Watson testified that she believes most citizens are aware of the complaint process, but "I believe . . . that there is a lack of confidence in the process, particularly with regard to black citizens.").

142   See, e.g., Testimony of David Honig, general counsel, Miami-Dade Branch, NAACP, Miami Hearings, November 12, 1991, at 175.

143   Id. at 171–75. The Miami-Dade Branch had received 75 complaints of police misconduct during this period, of which 21 were made by persons who gave their names and sufficient details to determine the complaints were "justified" and should be investigated. In the 2 cases presented to the police, the complaints were not resolved successfully; the police departments took the information and never contacted the NAACP to respond to the allegations. Id.

144   Testimony of John W. Mack, Urban League, Los Angeles Hearings, December 3, 1991, 3:00 p.m., at 82. See also Testimony of David Honig, general counsel, Miami-Dade Branch, NAACP, Miami Hearings, November 12, 1991, at 175 ("Most instances of police misconduct are never reported to the NAACP.").

145   See, e.g., Testimony of Rev. Joseph Green, vice-mayor, City of Norfolk, Norfolk Hearings, November 6, 1991, at 28 ("There is a formalized complaint system within the police department . . . but the citizens [sic] who calls is not aware of it."); Testimony of Mary Redd, Urban League, Norfolk Hearings, November 6, 1991, at 180; Testimony of Ms. White, Norfolk Hearings, November 6, 1991, at 181; Testimony of George E. Mins, president, Virginia Beach NAACP, Norfolk Hearings, November 6, 1991, at 181. In contrast, some police officials testified they believed most citizens know they can call and file a complaint. See, e.g., Testimony of Maj. Dennis R. Long, St. Louis County Police Department, St. Louis Hearings, December 6, 1991, at 29.

146   See, e.g., Testimony of Chief Charles Wall, Virginia Beach Police Department, Norfolk Hearings, November 6, 1991, at 48 (testifying that complaints may be made to a supervisor at any precinct and that complainants may also call a 24-hour hotline or an emergency number); Testimony of Chief Elizabeth Watson, Houston Police Department, Houston Hearings, November 19, 1991, at 24–25 (testifying that a complaint can be filed at any police facility: "Any supervisor, anywhere, even an officer, is required to make known any allegation of misconduct that is presented to him by a citizen.").

147   See, e.g., Testimony of Maj. Dennis R. Long, St. Louis County Police Department, St. Louis Hearings, December 6, 1991, at 24; Testi-

mony of Clarence Fisher, superintendent, Missouri State Highway Patrol, St. Louis Hearings, December 6, 1991, at 30 ("[I]f they ask an officer, they'll be instructed how to file a complaint."); Testimony of Col. William H. Young, St. Louis Black Leadership Round Table, St. Louis Hearings, December 6, 1991, at 69–70 (testifying that officers of the St. Louis Police Department do not have the authority to reject a complaint, because official policy of the department is to receive and process every complaint).

148   See, e.g., Testimony of Clarence Fisher, superintendent, Missouri State Highway Patrol, St. Louis Hearings, December 6, 1991, at 23 (testifying that a pamphlet is sent to anyone who calls about a complaint); Testimony of Chief Clarence Harmon, St. Louis Metropolitan Police Department, St. Louis Hearings, December 6, 1991, at 50.

149   See, e.g., Testimony of Helen Gros, executive director, Texas ACLU, Houston Hearings, November 19, 1991, at 197; Testimony of Sylvia Brooks, president, Houston Urban League, Houston Hearings, November 19, 1991, at 178.

150   See, e.g., Testimony of Joseph Johnson, Indianapolis Hearings, December 17, 1991, at 408; Testimony of Joyce Armstrong, ACLU, St. Louis Hearings, December 6, 1991, at 62; Testimony of James Beauford, Urban League, Metropolitan St. Louis, St. Louis Hearings, December 6, 1991, at 45; Testimony of John Williams, Miami Hearings, November 12, 1991, at 162.

151   See, e.g., Testimony of Sylvia Brooks, president, Houston Urban League, Houston Hearings, November 19, 1991, at 177–78 ("I would think most people don't know exactly what to [do] when they want to make a complaint."); Testimony of Helen Gros, executive director, Texas ACLU, Houston Hearings, November 19, 1991, at 178 ("My experience is that the general citizens who call my office do not have a clue . . . that there is an Internal Affairs Division. . . ."); Testimony of Elutero Roman, Miami Hearings, November 12, 1991, at 316.

152   See, e.g., Testimony of Rev. Willie Simms, Metro-Dade Community Affairs, Black Affairs Program, Miami Hearings, November 13, 1991, at 63.

153   See, e.g., Testimony of Joyce Armstrong, ACLU, St. Louis Hearings, December 6, 1991, at 62.

154   Testimony of Chief Clarence Harmon, St. Louis Metropolitan Police Department, St. Louis Hearings, December 6, 1991, at 50.

155   The Christopher Commission contacted a sample of former complainants. It discovered that both those whose complaints had been sustained and those whose complaints had been "not sustained" reported they had been discouraged or intimidated from making complaints. Christopher Commission Report, at 158–59.

156   See, e.g., Testimony of George E. Mins, president, Virginia Beach NAACP, Norfolk Hearings, November 6, 1991, at 8. The Christopher Commission found that some officers recorded complaints in daily logs rather

than on the official complaint forms, which generate investigations. CHRISTOPHER COMMISSION REPORT, at 159.

157   *See* discussion of retaliatory practices of the police, *supra* at 40–42, Finding B4.

158   *See* Testimony of Lawrence Graves, ST. LOUIS HEARINGS, December 6, 1991, at 90–94.

159   *See* Testimony of George E. Mins, president, Virginia Beach NAACP, NORFOLK HEARINGS, November 6, 1991, at 7 (testifying that the NAACP observer had been attacked by the police, handcuffed on the ground, and attacked by police dogs); Testimony of Bernard T. Holmes, legal counsel, Virginia Beach NAACP, NORFOLK HEARINGS, November 6, 1991, at 58–73.

160   *See* Testimony of Helen Gros, executive director, Texas ACLU, HOUSTON HEARINGS, November 19, 1991, at 157–59 (testifying that the woman indicted was a well-known community activist who had previously had public disagreements with the officer involved).

161   *See* Myron W. Orfield, Jr., *Deterrence, Perjury, and the Heater Factor: An Exclusionary Rule in the Chicago Criminal Courts,* 63 U. COLO. L. REV. 75 (1992) (describing routine police perjury in suppression hearings in Chicago courts).

162   *See id.*

163   *See* Testimony of Joanne Moody, ST. LOUIS HEARINGS, December 6, 1991, at 108–12.

164   *See* Testimony of Joyce Armstrong, ACLU, ST. LOUIS HEARINGS, December 6, 1991, at 62.

165   Testimony of David Shaheed, president-elect, Marion County Bar Association, INDIANAPOLIS HEARINGS, December 17, 1991, at 133–34 (testifying that the incidents were the shooting of a woman by two police officers who were trying to disarm her of a steak knife, the shooting of a young man after he was stopped for "riding his bicycle erratically," and the alleged suicide of a juvenile while handcuffed in the back seat of a police car).

166   *Roache Seeks Study of New Panel's Rules,* BOSTON GLOBE, June 27, 1992, at 15.

167   CHRISTOPHER COMMISSION REPORT, at 158.

168   *See, e.g,* Testimony of David Honig, general counsel, Miami-Dade Branch, NAACP, MIAMI HEARINGS, November 12, 1991, at 179; Testimony of Deborah Gordon, MIAMI HEARINGS, November 15, 1991, at 699.

169   *See, e.g,* Testimony of Mrs. Mitchell, MIAMI HEARINGS, November 13, 1991, at 555 (testifying that the police department said it would contact her later and that it needed to investigate before taking her complaint).

170   *See, e.g.,* Testimony of Bernard T. Holmes, legal counsel, Virginia Beach NAACP, NORFOLK HEARINGS, November 6, 1991, at 69–71 (recounting how, following a major incident in 1989 involving students in Virginia

Beach, police either refused to take complaints or discouraged them by telling complainants to come back next week, and pointing out that since most complainants were students and school was not then in session, few formal complaints were filed); Testimony of David Honig, general counsel, Miami-Dade branch, NAACP, MIAMI HEARINGS, November 12, 1991, at 179. *See also* CHRISTOPHER COMMISSION REPORT, at 158 (finding that intake officers in the LAPD discouraged filing complaints by being uncooperative and by requiring long waits to complete the complaint forms and that there were no Spanish-speaking officers to take complaints in areas with large Latino populations).

171   *See, e.g.,* Testimony of Rev. Willie Simms, Metro-Dade Community Affairs, Black Affairs Program, MIAMI HEARINGS, November 12, 1991, at 65-66.

172   Testimony of Vincent Calhoun, LOS ANGELES HEARINGS, December 3, 1991, at 139.

173   *See, e.g.,* Testimony of Jeanette Amadeo, MIAMI HEARINGS, November 13, 1991, at 688; Testimony of Judy Steen Davis, MIAMI HEARINGS, November 13, 1991, at 565 ("When you go before the . . . Police Department and you make a claim . . . they place a gag order on you so that you can't speak publicly about it. They don't want you saying things.").

174   *See* Testimony of Ernest Fields, ST. LOUIS HEARINGS, December 6, 1991, at 92.

175   *Id.* at 88–89.

176   *See, e.g.,* Testimony of Dr. Willie Williams, Fair Share Job Committee of PULSE, MIAMI HEARINGS, November 13, 1991, at 494–95.

177   *See, e.g., id.* at 495.

178   *See, e.g.,* Testimony of Ms. White, NORFOLK HEARINGS, November 6, 1991, at 161; Statement of Ms. Smith, HOUSTON HEARINGS, November 19, 1991, at 322–23 (testifying that student witnesses to the shooting of Byron Gillum felt "intimidated away from providing facts during that investigation . . . [and] felt that they were being discredited in their testimony . . . to the point where they wanted to shy away from the investigation itself.").

179   The Christopher Commission found that the greatest number of adverse complaints about the LAPD concerned the handling of complaints against its officers, particularly those involving the excessive use of force. CHRISTOPHER COMMISSION REPORT, at 153.

180   *See, e.g.,* Testimony of William P. Robinson, member of the Virginia House of Delegates, NORFOLK HEARINGS, November 6, 1991, at 120 (stating that the internal affairs process of handling complaints has been ineffective). *See also* Testimony of Mary Redd, Urban League, NORFOLK HEARINGS, November 6, 1991, at 147 ("[Internal Affairs] is not really the answer to solving the problems [of misconduct].").

181   *See, e.g.,* Testimony of William P. Robinson, member of the Virginia House of Delegates, Norfolk Hearings, November 6, 1991, at 122–23.

182   Testimony of Dr. Willie Williams, Fair Share Job Committee of PULSE, Miami Hearings, November 13, 1991, at 493–94.

183   *See, e.g.,* Testimony of David Perkins, Miami Hearings, November 13, 1991, at 671, 693–94 (Mr. Perkins, an African American man, testified: "It doesn't do no good [to complain] because they doesn't do their proper investigation. When anybody go[es] to file their complaint by an officer, they do not come out in the community to do any investigation to find out the new facts of what actually occurred. Only thing they do is wait until the officer can be contacted. . . . They tell a lie face-to-face. That whole entire department backs him up one hundred percent. . . . [A]ll the law enforcement departments are constantly doing this."); Testimony of Henry Paxton, attorney for the Henry Peco Justice Committee, Los Angeles Hearings, December 3, 1991, at 164 (testifying that after the fatal shooting of Henry Peco, police did not interview witnesses until four days after the incident); St. Clair Commission Report, at 109 (its review of 257 Boston Police Department internal affairs cases revealed that no witnesses were contacted by any police personnel in 79% of the cases).

184   *See, e.g.,* Testimony of George E. Mins, president, Virginia Beach NAACP, Norfolk Hearings, November 6, 1991, at 178–79 (regarding NAACP review of internal affairs investigations in Virginia Beach). *See also* St. Clair Commission Report, at iii (The commission's review of the Boston Police Department's internal affairs investigations of citizen complaints revealed "an investigative and hearing process characterized by shoddy, halfhearted investigations, lengthy delays and inadequate documentation and record-keeping."). *See also* Christopher Commission Report, at 161 (finding that in the cases where officers were involved in shootings, officers were interviewed as a group and statements were recorded only after a "pre-interview" was completed).

185   *See* Christopher Commission Report, at 163.

186   *See* Testimony of Joyce Armstrong, ACLU, St. Louis Hearings, December 6, 1991, at 66–67 (testifying some witnesses do not want to say anything, but in most cases there are no witnesses); Testimony of Chief Ian Shipley, Chesapeake Police Department, Norfolk Hearings, November 6, 1991, at 63 (testifying most of the complaints involve one-on-one confrontations, without witnesses). *See also* St. Clair Commission Report, at 100 (finding that there were rarely witnesses in the internal affairs cases of the Boston Police Department); Christopher Commission Report, at ii (concluding that it was doubtful there would have been a police investigation or that any investigation would have sustained a complaint of police misconduct were it not for the videotape in the Rodney King case).

187   *See, e.g.,* Testimony of Joyce Armstrong, ACLU, St. Louis Hearings, December 6, 1991, at 59.

188   *See, e.g.,* Testimony of Fred Taylor, director, Metro-Dade Police

Department, MIAMI HEARINGS, November 12, 1991, at 85 (testifying that in one-third of the cases there are not enough facts to say whether the officer or the civilian is right and these result in a non-sustained finding, and that the department tracks all complaints but pays particular attention to those that are not sustained). *See also* CHRISTOPHER COMMISSION REPORT, at 155 (finding that excessive-force and improper-tactics complaints were rarely sustained in the LAPD investigations unless there were noninvolved, independent witnesses who corroborated the complainant's story). This pattern of accused officers prevailing when a "mere citizen" is the accuser in an internal investigation is another version of what civilian accusers routinely experience when they find themselves charged with crimes in connection with alleged police misconduct. Again, even when the standard of proof is "beyond a reasonable doubt," the word of a police officer suffices.

189   *See* CHRISTOPHER COMMISSION REPORT, at 155 (finding that complaints almost invariably were "not sustained" when the only witnesses were the officer and the complainant or friends or family of the complainant).

190   *Id.* at 153.

191   Testimony of Neil F. Kurlander, chief of police, Maryland Heights, Missouri, ST. LOUIS HEARINGS, December 6, 1991, at 102 (Kurlander testified that there are ways to change this situation, including tracking all complaints and all cases of assault, whether by officers or by citizens, and making regular reviews of the information. "It doesn't take a brain surgeon to figure out that if everybody is doing the same job why is one officer getting more complaints than everybody else. That's the administrator's job, to look at that to get the officer and change his attitude, give him more training or get rid of him. It's that simple.").

192   *See, e.g.,* Testimony of George E. Mins, president, Virginia Beach NAACP, NORFOLK HEARINGS, November 6, 1991, at 168 (The police have an attitude of "you have a criminal record so we don't need to credit what you're saying.").

193   *See, e.g.,* Testimony of William P. Robinson, member of the Virginia House of Delegates, NORFOLK HEARINGS, November 6, 1991, at 121.

194   Testimony of Ms. White, NORFOLK HEARINGS, November 6, 1991, at 160–61.

195   Testimony of George E. Mins, president, Virginia Beach NAACP, NORFOLK HEARINGS, November 6, 1991, at 168–69.

196   CHRISTOPHER COMMISSION REPORT, at 162.

197   *Id.* at 162–63. At the same time, police officers at the scene are usually viewed as "independent" witnesses. *Id.*

198   *See, e.g.,* Testimony of Maj. Dennis R. Long, St. Louis County Police Department, ST. LOUIS HEARINGS, December 6, 1991, at 15 (testifying that the complainant receives written findings at end of investigation if officer is exonerated); Testimony of Chief Clarence Harmon, St. Louis

Metropolitan Police Department, St. Louis Hearings, December 6, 1991, at 42 (testifying that the complainant gets notification within 15 days that the police department has the complaint and is investigating, and that internal affairs is to complete its investigation within 30 days, unless there are extenuating circumstances; complainant gets immediate notification of the recommended findings and the right to appeal in person to the board of police commissioners to present new evidence or information that the police department did not adequately investigate).

In some jurisdictions, the police department can tell a citizen his or her complaint has been sustained and "appropriate action" has been taken, but, because of a Peace Officer Bill of Rights, cannot disclose what the "appropriate action was or how far it went." *See* Testimony of Richard L. Foreman, assistant sheriff, Los Angeles County Sheriff's Department, Los Angeles Hearings, December 4, 1991, at 22–24. *See also* Testimony of Chief Lawrence L. Binkley, Long Beach Police Department, Los Angeles Hearings, December 4, 1991, at 91 (testifying that he has been advised by the city attorney that he can disclose to the public that the department has terminated *an* officer as a result of a shooting, but cannot disclose the termination of a *specific* officer before a public civil service hearing is held).

199   *See* Testimony of David Honig, general counsel, Miami-Dade Branch, NAACP, Miami Hearings, November 12, 1991, at 171–75. *See also* St. Clair Commission Report, at 120 (finding that in Boston no notice is given to the complainant regarding the status of his or her complaint).

200   *See, e.g.,* Testimony of Dr. Willie Williams, Fair Share Job Committee of PULSE, Miami Hearings, November 13, 1991, at 496–97 (testifying that investigations take months, sometimes years). *See also* St. Clair Commission Report, at 118 (finding that the most frequent complaint about the IAD process was delay, and that in many cases they reviewed a complaint was eventually designated not sustained due to lack of a witness).

201   *See, e.g.,* Testimony of Mary Redd, Urban League, Norfolk Hearings, November 6, 1991, at 150–51 (testifying that people have been telling her for years they make a complaint and "virtually nothing happens"; for example, two of her students had gone to internal affairs to complain about police treatment and "nothing happened [with it].").

202   *See* Testimony of Judy Steen Davis, Miami Hearings, November 13, 1991, at 564–65.

203   Testimony of Chief Ian Shipley, Chesapeake Police Department, Norfolk Hearings, November 6, 1991, at 38–39.

204   *Id.* at 42–43, 63–64.

205   Testimony of Chief Lawrence L. Binkley, Long Beach Police Department, Los Angeles Hearings, December 4, 1991, at 65.

206   Testimony of Chief Michael R. McCrary, Signal Hill Police De-

partment, Los Angeles County, LOS ANGELES HEARINGS, December 4, 1991, at 130.

207 *Id.* at 131.

208 *See, e.g.,* Testimony of Dr. Willie Williams, Fair Share Job Committee of PULSE, MIAMI HEARINGS, November 13, 1991, at 493, 497 (testifying that the police internal review is usually a whitewash); Testimony of David Perkins, MIAMI HEARINGS, November 13, 1991, at 693–94; Testimony of Kathleen Worthy, UP-PAC, MIAMI HEARINGS, November 13, 1991, at 479 ("There have been many Rodney King cases in Dade County, which were not videotaped. Most of them are white-washed by internal affairs."); Testimony of Lawrence Graves, ST. LOUIS HEARINGS, December 6, 1991, at 93–94 (testifying that average citizens do not have confidence in the complaint process because they feel they are outnumbered); Testimony of Mary May Dixon, HOUSTON HEARINGS, November 19, 1991, at 420–21 (testifying that she does not have confidence that the IAD investigation of her complaint regarding the police shooting of her son will be given serious consideration); Testimony of Michael Genson, HOUSTON HEARINGS, November 19, 1991, at 422 (testifying that he was beaten by police when he urinated in an alleyway, then arrested for resisting arrest, and that he has no confidence his complaint will be taken seriously).

209 *See, e.g.,* Testimony of Ms. White, NORFOLK HEARINGS, November 6, 1991, at 183.

210 *See, e.g.,* Testimony of Chief Lawrence L. Binkley, Long Beach Police Department, LOS ANGELES HEARINGS, December 4, 1991, at 65 (testifying that an investigation revealed his department was reluctant to take personnel complaints that might result in a demotion of supervisors).

211 *See, e.g.,* Testimony of Carol Heppe, director, Police Watch, LOS ANGELES HEARINGS, December 4, 1991, at 151 ("[I]f you look at how that department [Internal Affairs] runs, an officer is put in that department for two or three years and then transferred. We cannot expect an officer who expects to be transferred in two or three years back into the police department to go after police officers who violate people's rights. They still have a career ahead of them. . . .").

212 *See, e.g.,* Testimony of George E. Mins, president, Virginia Beach NAACP, NORFOLK HEARINGS, November 6, 1991, at 167–68. *Compare with* Testimony of Dr. Larry Capp, psychologist, MIAMI HEARINGS, November 12, 1991, at 231 (testifying that the police department will not fail to follow his recommendations for counseling of officers because the police would expose themselves to liability if the officer subsequently engaged in misconduct).

213 *See* Testimony of Chief Charles Wall, Virginia Beach Police Department, NORFOLK HEARINGS, November 6, 1991, at 48 (did not specify the period in which the complaints were made).

214 *See* Testimony of Maj. Dennis R. Long, St. Louis County Police Department, ST. LOUIS HEARINGS, December 6, 1991, at 13.

215   *Id.*

216   *See* Testimony of Fred Taylor, director, Metro-Dade Police Department, MIAMI HEARINGS, November 12, 1991, at 84–85 (testifying that in the second third of the complaint cases the officers acted in good faith and the parties end up agreeing there was a misunderstanding, and that in the remaining third there are insufficient facts to determine whether the officer or the citizen is right). Taylor did not testify whether the sustained rate varied depending upon whether the complaint was made by a citizen or arose within the department. *Id.*

217   Unauthorized-force complaints represented between 13.5% and 15.5% of the total number of complaints during each year of this period. *See* written materials submitted by Metro-Dade Police Department, "Allegations of Unauthorized Force to Total Complaints Received Comparison," Section 1, Miami Hearings, November 12–13, 1991.

218   *See* written materials submitted by Metro-Dade Police Department, "Sustained Cases of Unauthorized Force," Section 1, MIAMI HEARINGS, November 12–13, 1991. Discipline imposed in these cases consisted of 1 counseling, 9 written reprimands, 7 suspensions ranging from 1 to 10 days, 2 resignations, and 2 terminations. *Id.*

219   CHRISTOPHER COMMISSION REPORT, at 153.

220   ST. CLAIR COMMISSION REPORT, at 115.

221   *Id.* at 106–7. The St. Clair Commission found that complaints of physical abuse constituted the most common complaint of misconduct—30.5%. *Id.* at 107.

222   *Id.* at 115. The Boston Police Department was the complainant in only 4% of the cases, most of which alleged violations of police department rules and regulations; a few alleged serious corruption. *Id.* at 108–9, 115.

223   *See* Testimony of John Mack, Urban League, LOS ANGELES HEARINGS, December 3, 1991, at 80–81.

224   *See id.* at 41–42 (testifying that a newspaper investigative story showed that "relatively minor departmental infractions . . . [were] more important than if someone beat someone half to death," and that in one case described, an officer who wore a pager in contravention of departmental policy "got 60 days," whereas the majority of officers found guilty of brutality receive less harsh penalties). *See also* Testimony of Gerald Cunningham, INDIANAPOLIS HEARINGS, December 17, 1991, at 295 ("[A] number of police officers are suspended, get reprimanded for very minor stuff. It's . . . like a military operation where tardiness and some minor infractions are regarded much more seriously [than] police abuse especially in black and Hispanic communities.").

225   *Id.* at 81.

226   ST. CLAIR COMMISSION REPORT, at 115. The status of civilian complainants of police misconduct is analogous to the traditional perception of rape complainants. Women used to be routinely discredited in rape

cases. Now there is a perception that women willing to come forward must be credible. One can hope for a similar evolution in the perception of the credibility of a citizen who complains of police abuse.

227   See, e.g., Testimony of David Shaheed, president-elect, Marion County Bar Association, INDIANAPOLIS HEARINGS, December 17, 1991, at 132–33 ("In talking to one of my colleagues . . . he admitted he doesn't handle police harassment and brutality cases any more. In all honesty the typical cases are an economic dilemma or disaster for most lawyers.").

228   See id. at 133 ("Most clients can't afford the retainer that should be required in the case based on the length of time it takes to get a recovery.").

229   See id. at 133 ("If you take the case on a contingent fee, it's essentially a crap shoot.").

230   See Testimony of Alexander Kelly, MIAMI HEARINGS, November 13, 1991, at 679–84 ([retired U.S. Army sergeant first class] testifying that while watching a peaceful Haitian demonstration, the police came from behind him, grabbed him, hit him in the groin and stomach, pulled his hair, and dragged him across the street. When he produced identification, he was told "Oh, you [are] old enough to remember when we used to beat the shit out of niggers. I want you to stand here, watch how we beat these niggers out there." He was put on a bus, taken to jail, and charged with inciting a riot. He testified that although he was found not guilty, he continued to be harassed by the same police. He complained to the civilian review board, but he had not heard anything in a year regarding his complaint.).

231   See, e.g., Testimony of David Shaheed, president-elect, Marion County Bar Association, INDIANAPOLIS HEARINGS, December 18, 1991, at 133.

232   See, e.g., Testimony of Anthony Moss, attorney, former public defender, MIAMI HEARINGS, November 13, 1991, at 593–603.

233   Id. at 601 (testifying that Florida sovereign immunity statutes limit awards to $100,000).

234   See, e.g., Testimony of David Shaheed, president-elect, Marion County Bar Association, representing African American lawyers in Marion County, INDIANAPOLIS HEARINGS, December 17, 1991, at 133 ("You are litigating against the party with substantially more resources."); Testimony of Anthony Moss, attorney, former public defender, MIAMI HEARINGS, November 13, 1991, at 593–603.

235   Testimony of David Shaheed, president-elect, Marion County Bar Association, INDIANAPOLIS HEARINGS, December 17, 1991, at 138.

236   In a televised joint interview of the jury forepersons in the two trials in the Rodney King case, the foreman in the second trial of the officers (on federal civil rights charges) stated that the video was the key factor in their verdicts. He stated that the enhancement of the video convinced the second jury that there were blows to King's head and that continued beating occurred after King did "everything he [could] do to

surrender." The forewoman of the jury in the first trial of the officers (on state charges) stated that, not having the more technologically advanced video enhancements used in the second trial, the jury "never saw an actual blow to the head. . . . Had we been able to see that, it probably would have made a great deal of difference in our verdict, because a blow to the head would have been deadly force, in our opinion."

Significantly, the jury foreman in the second trial stated that he did not find King a compelling witness, asserting, "[T]here really was no evidence . . . that he presented that I would say would convict anybody of any crimes, for sure." The jury forewoman in the first trial commented, "[T]here really was not that much difference in the verdicts. We both found Officers Wind and Briseno not guilty." "ABC News Nightline" (ABC Television broadcast, April 27, 1993).

Note also the recent result in the widely publicized prosecution of police officer Rene Lozano. Though in 1989 a multiethnic jury convicted him of manslaughter in the shooting of an African American man in Miami, when that verdict was overturned prosecutors were unable to secure a conviction in the retrial. *See Miami Police Officer Is Acquitted in Racially Charged Slaying Case*, N.Y. TIMES, May 29, 1993, at A1.

237   *See* Testimony of Joyce Armstrong, ACLU, ST. LOUIS HEARINGS, December 6, 1991, at 59.

238   Testimony of George E. Mins, president, Virginia Beach NAACP, NORFOLK HEARINGS, November 6, 1991, at 6.

239   Testimony of Rev. Jew Don Boney, National Black United Front, HOUSTON HEARINGS, November 19, 1991, at 428.

240   *See* Testimony of Rickie Clark, National Black Police Association, INDIANAPOLIS HEARINGS, December 17, 1991, at 289.

241   *See* Testimony of Bernard T. Holmes, legal counsel, Virginia Beach NAACP, NORFOLK HEARINGS, November 6, 1991, at 77.

242   *See* Testimony of Diane Watson, California state senator, LOS ANGELES HEARINGS, December 3, 1991, at 19.

243   *Id.* at 19–20.

244   *See* Testimony of Carol Heppe, director, Police Watch, LOS ANGELES HEARINGS, December 4, 1991, at 154.

245   *Id.*

246   *Id.* at 153.

247   *See* Testimony of James Beauford, Urban League, Metropolitan St. Louis, ST. LOUIS HEARINGS, December 6, 1991, at 44.

248   *See id.* at 44.

249   Testimony of Col. William H. Young, St. Louis Black Leadership Round Table, ST. LOUIS HEARINGS, December 6, 1991, at 69.

250   Testimony of Herman E. Springs, director of police, Norfolk State University, NORFOLK HEARINGS, November 6, 1991, at 45.

251   A series of articles in the BOSTON GLOBE, in August 1992, outlined allegations by minority officers in the Boston Police Department that a

"racial double standard" is part of the "daily routine." *See Boston Minority Officers Charge Double Standard,* BOSTON GLOBE, Aug. 2, 1992, at 1, 24 (A black woman officer interviewed is reported to have said: "They say there's a 'code of blue' in the Police Department. . . . It's not a code of blue. It's a code of white."). *See also Boston Officer Backs Bias Call,* BOSTON GLOBE, Aug. 3, 1992, at 14, and *Ex-Officer Says Roots in Community Cost Him Job,* BOSTON GLOBE, Aug. 4, 1992, at 13.

252   Testimony of Herman E. Springs, director of police, Norfolk State University, NORFOLK HEARINGS, November 6, 1991, at 44–45.

253   PETER MAAS, SERPICO (1973).

254   *See, e.g.,* Testimony of Clarence Fisher, superintendent, Missouri State Highway Patrol, ST. LOUIS HEARINGS, December 6, 1991, at 27 (Denying the existence of a code, Fisher stated, "We have very strict performing requirements and they are in force.").

255   *See, e.g.,* Testimony of Msgr. Brian Walsh, Catholic Commission for Social Advocacies, MIAMI HEARINGS, November 12, 1991, at 192 (testifying that the need for an esprit de corps is carried to extremes by some police officers, who protect fellow officers at all costs). *See also* Testimony of Janet Reno, Dade County state's attorney, MIAMI HEARINGS, November 12, 1991, at 18–19 (testifying that police officers have told her that there is a code of silence, but some officers have cooperated in prosecutions of fellow officers; the code of silence constantly arises as an issue that has to be addressed).

256   Testimony of Rodney Williams, chairman, Ethical Society of Police, ST. LOUIS HEARINGS, December 6, 1991, at 76.

257   *Wave of Abuse Claims Laid to a Few Officers,* BOSTON GLOBE, Oct. 4, 1992, at 1, 28, 29.

258   *See, e.g.,* Testimony of Chief Ian Shipley, Chesapeake Police Department, NORFOLK HEARINGS, November 6, 1991, at 68–69; Testimony of Mayor William Ward, Chesapeake, NORFOLK HEARINGS, November 6, 1991, at 111.

259   Testimony of Chief Charles Wall, Virginia Beach Police Department, NORFOLK HEARINGS, November 6, 1991, at 69.

260   *See, e.g.,* Testimony of Chief Ian Shipley, Chesapeake Police Department, NORFOLK HEARINGS, November 6, 1991, at 68.

261   *See, e.g.,* Testimony of Rev. Joseph Green, vice-mayor, City of Norfolk, NORFOLK HEARINGS, November 6, 1991, at 22 ("I think that atmosphere is still there and hope it is getting less and less, but we are trying to work with it. . . ."); Testimony of Mayor William Ward, Chesapeake, NORFOLK HEARINGS, November 6, 1991, at 102, 113 (testifying that there are isolated complaints from citizens, but the department has been sensitized, and that citizen complaints are typically for discourteous behavior, compared to complaints of brutality in the 1970s and 1980s).

262   *See, e.g.,* Testimony of T. Willard Fair, president, Urban League of Greater Miami, MIAMI HEARINGS, November 12, 1991, at 150–51 (testify-

ing that he feels there is neither tolerance nor policies nor condoning of excessive force in Miami, and that the new police administration has tried to improve the force's image in the community by using walking police, salt-and-pepper teams, ministations, and substations).

263   *See, e.g.,* Testimony of Maj. Sheldon Darden, chief of operations, Norfolk Police Department, NORFOLK HEARINGS, November 6, 1991, at 59.

264   *See, e.g.,* Testimony of Mabel Edmonds, ST. LOUIS HEARINGS, December 6, 1991, at 84–88; Testimony of Arnetta Kelly, ST. LOUIS HEARINGS, December 6, 1991, at 81–83; Testimony of John E. Williams, MIAMI HEARINGS, November 12, 1991, at 155–66; Testimony of William P. Robinson, member of the Virginia House of Delegates, NORFOLK HEARINGS, November 6, 1991, at 125; Testimony of Dr. Helen Green, NORFOLK HEARINGS, November 6, 1991, at 12–13.

265   *See, e.g.,* Testimony of William P. Robinson, member of the Virginia House of Delegates, NORFOLK HEARINGS, November 6, 1991, at 125; Testimony of Dr. Helen Green, NORFOLK HEARINGS, November 6, 1991, at 12–13 (testifying that although there has been improvement in the last 25 years because of professionalization of the police, an increase in the number of black officers, especially as executives, and Supreme Court decisions emphasizing individual rights, ". . . yet police violence and corruption, though not pervasive, continue to exist").

266   Testimony of Rickie Clark, National Black Police Association, INDIANAPOLIS HEARINGS, December 18, 1991, at 259.

267   Testimony of Rodney Williams, chairman, Ethical Society of Police, ST. LOUIS HEARINGS, December 6, 1991, at 71.

268   *See* Testimony of Shelby Lanier, chairman, National Black Police Association, INDIANAPOLIS HEARINGS, December 18, 1991, at 271.

269   *See* Testimony of Ernie Neal, vice-president, Miami chapter of NOBLE, MIAMI HEARINGS, November 13, 1991, at 610–11 (testifying that NOBLE was founded about 1979 by 10 African American law-enforcement executives in order to "educate young executives just entering the field . . . just making the ranks of sergeant and captain . . . they needed additional training in how to succeed to become Chief . . . a lot of our black Chiefs . . . are members. . . . We do . . . training, conferences, workshops . . . [and] we plan on bring[ing] the community into that training. . . .").

270   Testimony of Herman E. Springs, director of police, Norfolk State University, NORFOLK HEARINGS, November 6, 1991, at 23.

271   Testimony of Ernie Neal, vice-president, Miami chapter of NOBLE, MIAMI HEARINGS, November 13, 1991, at 579.

272   *See* Testimony of Herman E. Springs, director of police, Norfolk State University, NORFOLK HEARINGS, November 6, 1991, at 23.

273   *See, e.g.,* Testimony of Ernie Neal, vice-president, Miami chapter of NOBLE, MIAMI HEARINGS, November 13, 1991, at 579–80.

274   *See, e.g.,* Testimony of Herman E. Springs, director of police, Norfolk State University, NORFOLK HEARINGS, November 6, 1991, at 26; Testimony of Shelby Lanier, chairman, National Black Police Association, INDIANAPOLIS HEARINGS, December 18, 1991, at 275.

275　Testimony of Rodney Williams, chairman, Ethical Society of Police, St. Louis Hearings, December 6, 1991, at 71.

276　*See* Testimony of Herman E. Springs, director of police, Norfolk State University, Norfolk Hearings, November 6, 1991, at 20.

277　*See* Testimony of Shelby Lanier, chairman, National Black Police Association, Indianapolis Hearings, December 18, 1991, at 275.

278　*See, e.g.,* Testimony of Doug Elder, president, Houston Police Officers' Association, Houston Hearings, November 20, 1991, at 65 (testifying that there is no code of silence now); Testimony of Chief Ian Shipley, Chesapeake Police Department, Norfolk Hearings, November 6, 1991, at 88–90 (testifying that police officers cannot keep quiet and any incidents would "go around the department" and that the code of silence really does not happen in their profession to any large extent); Testimony of Clarence Fisher, superintendent, Missouri State Highway Patrol, St. Louis Hearings, December 6, 1991, at 27–28 (testifying that, having been an officer for 33 years, he had not heard of the code of silence within his department and that his department had very strict performing requirements in the use of force); Testimony of Maj. Dennis R. Long, St. Louis County Police Department, St. Louis Hearings, December 6, 1991, at 27 (testifying that, having been an officer for 32 years, he had never seen evidence of a code of silence within his department).

279　*See, e.g.,* Testimony of Chief Charles Wall, Virginia Beach Police Department, Norfolk Hearings, November 6, 1991, at 90 ("I think there's some reluctance among police officers to talk about other police officers. . . .").

280　*See, e.g.,* Testimony of Neil F. Kurlander, Board of Governors for Law Enforcement Officials of Greater St. Louis, St. Louis Hearings, December 6, 1991, at 107 (testifying that the code of silence did exist, but he had not seen that type of behavior to a large extent in the last 10–15 years and that the code is more prevalent in larger police departments and among the older generation of police officers).

281　*See, e.g.,* Testimony of Fred Taylor, director, Metro-Dade Police Department, Miami Hearings, November 12, 1991, at 115–16 (testifying that the code of silence did and may still exist, and that "[y]ou don't have room on the force for those kinds of individuals. I think once you make it clear that is not a sensitive way to behave that if you do that you are not too well to come [*sic*] on the force and you take action.").

282　*See id.*

283　Testimony of Don Smyth, Houston Hearings, November 19, 1991, at 313–14.

284　*See, e.g.,* Testimony of Rodney Williams, chairman, Ethical Society of Police, St. Louis Hearings, December 6, 1991, at 74; Testimony of May Walker, African-American Police Officers League, Houston Hearings, November 20, 1991, at 94, 98; Testimony of Herman E. Springs, director of police, Norfolk State University, Norfolk Hearings, November 6, 1991, at 34.

285　See, e.g., Testimony of Herman E. Springs, director of police, Norfolk State University, Norfolk Hearings, November 6, 1991, at 48; Testimony of Migdaly Rivas, Miami Hearings, November 13, 1991, at 635 ("Routine altering of arrest forms to suit the letter of the law . . . was joked [about] as creative writing.").

286　See Testimony of Herman E. Springs, director of police, Norfolk State University, Norfolk Hearings, November 6, 1991, at 34.

287　See, e.g., Testimony of May Walker, African-American Police Officers League, Houston Hearings, November 20, 1991, at 94, 98.

288　See, e.g., Testimony of Mary Redd, Urban League, Norfolk Hearings, November 6, 1991, at 155; Testimony of Herman E. Springs, director of police, Norfolk State University, Norfolk Hearings, November 6, 1991, at 30 (testifying that he anticipates a backlash against African American officers who report police abuse, resulting in disciplinary complaints against them for interfering with an arrest or conduct unbecoming an officer).

289　See Testimony of Herman E. Springs, director of police, Norfolk State University, Norfolk Hearings, November 6, 1991, at 45 (testifying that his complaint to his police superiors about the beating of an African American teenager led to his responding to calls on his own, and without backup, in precarious situations).

290　Testimony of Migdaly Rivas, Miami Hearings, November 13, 1991, at 633.

291　Id. at 634, 636.

292　Testimony of May Walker, African-American Police Officers League, Houston Hearings, November 20, 1991, at 94, 98.

293　Christopher Commission Report, at 170.

294　See Testimony of Herman E. Springs, director of police, Norfolk State University, Norfolk Hearings, November 6, 1991, at 30.

295　See, e.g., Testimony of Chief Ian Shipley, Chesapeake Police Department, Norfolk Hearings, November 6, 1991, at 88–90; Testimony of Chief Charles Wall, Virginia Beach Police Department, Norfolk Hearings, November 6, 1991, at 90–91 (testifying that in noncriminal matters he can order an officer to talk to him or to take a polygraph examination, and if an officer refuses to give a statement "they're gone").

296　See, e.g., Testimony of Maj. Sheldon Darden, chief of operations, Norfolk Police Department, Norfolk Hearings, November 6, 1991, at 92.

297　Even in departments where upper-echelon police officials described a philosophy of cooperation with and sensitivity to the community, police officials acknowledged the continuing prevalence of an "us versus them" attitude. See, e.g., Testimony of Assistant Chief Phyllis Wunsche, Houston Police Department, IAD, Houston Hearings, November 19, 1991, at 111 (testifying that some officers still may have a paramilitary kind of mentality, "us versus them," although the overall departmental philosophy of policing has changed); Testimony of Assistant Chief Jimmy L. Dotson, Houston Police Department, HOUSTON HEARINGS, November 19, 1991, at 138 (testifying that the administration of his department is trying to "aggressively manage and create an environment where those types of behaviors will not be tolerated"); Statement of Judge Green, HOUSTON HEARINGS, November 19, 1991, at 136 (testifying that after the conviction of a Hispanic officer for killing a black man, the patrolmen's association "insist[ed] that justice had not been done."). *Id.* at 138.

298   Testimony of Chief Elizabeth Watson, Houston Police Department, HOUSTON HEARINGS, November 19, 1991, at 4. Some police officials still offer arrest statistics as a key response to community problems. *See, e.g.,* Testimony of Fred Taylor, director, Metro-Dade Police Department, MIAMI HEARINGS, November 12, 1991, at 124, and written materials submitted by Metro-Dade Police Department (referring to the increase in Metro-Dade arrests as evidence of improvement in the response of his department, testified that Metro-Dade made 71,434 arrests in 1990, compared to 39,843 arrests in 1985, and that between 1980 and 1990 the number of sworn officers increased by 60%).

299   Testimony of Chief Elizabeth Watson, Houston Police Department, HOUSTON HEARINGS, November 19, 1991, at 3.

300   Testimony of Chief Clarence Harmon, St. Louis Metropolitan Police Department, ST. LOUIS HEARINGS, December 6, 1991, at 43.

301   Testimony of Maj. Dennis R. Long, St. Louis County Police Department, ST. LOUIS HEARINGS, December 6, 1991, at 33.

302   *See* Testimony of Clarence Fisher, superintendent, Missouri State Highway Patrol, ST. LOUIS HEARINGS, December 6, 1991, at 8.

303   Testimony of Fred Taylor, director, Metro-Dade Police Department, MIAMI HEARINGS, November 12, 1991, at 89.

304   Testimony of Chief Calvin Ross, Miami Police Department, MIAMI HEARINGS, November 13, 1991, at 441–42.

305   *See* Testimony of Chief Clarence Harmon, St. Louis Metropolitan Police Department, ST. LOUIS HEARINGS, December 6, 1991, at 52.

306   Testimony of Chief Elizabeth Watson, Houston Police Department, HOUSTON HEARINGS, November 19, 1991, at 4.

307   Testimony of Chief Calvin Ross, Miami Police Department, MIAMI HEARINGS, November 12, 1991, at 441–43.

308   Testimony of Col. David A. Robbins, president, Board of St. Louis Police Commissioners, ST. LOUIS HEARINGS, December 6, 1991, at 40.

309   Testimony of Chief Clarence Harmon, St. Louis Metropolitan Police Department, ST. LOUIS HEARINGS, December 6, 1991, at 43.

310   *See* Testimony of Chief Ian Shipley, Chesapeake Police Department, NORFOLK HEARINGS, November 6, 1991, at 43–45.

311   *Id.*

312   Testimony of Clarence Fisher, superintendent, Missouri State Highway Patrol, St. Louis Hearings, December 6, 1991, at 10.

313   Testimony of Maj. Dennis R. Long, St. Louis County Police Department, St. Louis Hearings, December 6, 1991, at 31.

314   *See* Testimony of Mayor William Ward, Norfolk Hearings, November 6, 1991, at 102–3 ("[F]or several years there we did have some charges of police brutality and, in fact, investigations revealed such, at which time the NAACP and other minority civic organizations protested and after which we had a series of meetings.").

315   Testimony of Rodney Williams, chairman, Ethical Society of Police, St. Louis Hearings, December 6, 1991, at 76.

316   Testimony of Maj. Dennis R. Long, St. Louis County Police Department, St. Louis Hearings, December 6, 1991, at 33.

317   Testimony of Shelby Lanier, chairman, National Black Police Association, Indianapolis Hearings, December 17, 1991, at 275.

318   Each of these cities had major incidents involving African American citizens and white police officers in late 1992 and 1993. *See, e.g.,* N.Y. Times, Nov. 18, 1992, at 1 (reporting the recent New York subway shooting of a black undercover police officer by fellow officers, who mistook him for a criminal); *Five Officers Probed in Beating of Black Policeman,* Boston Globe, Dec. 16, 1992, at 25 (reporting the beating of a black undercover officer by five white policemen during a traffic stop in Nashville).

319   *See* Testimony of Prof. Marvin Jones, University of Miami Law School, Miami Hearings, November 12, 1991, at 182–84.

320   Diane Watson, California State senator, Los Angeles Hearings, December 13, 1991, at 17.

321   *See, e.g.,* Testimony of John Pace, Miami Hearings, November 13, 1991, at 708.

322   *See, e.g.,* Testimony of Clemente Montalvo, Miami Hearings, November 12, 1991, at 324–25 (testifying that it would help to have more Puerto Rican officers patrolling his neighborhood); Testimony of Rolande Dorancy, executive director, Haitian Refugee Center, Miami Hearings, November 12, 1991, at 195 (testifying that she is concerned about the lack of Haitian Americans in the police department; more white officers patrol in the black community, which "can intimidate them.").

323   *See* Testimony of Dr. Larry Capp, psychologist, Miami Hearings, November 12, 1991, at 213–14.

324   Testimony of David Honig, general counsel, Miami-Dade Branch, NAACP, Miami Hearings, November 12, 1991, at 179.

325   *See* Testimony of Sam Jones, Urban League, Indianapolis Hearings, December 17, 1991, at 176.

326   *Id.*

327   *See, e.g.,* Testimony of Mayor William Hudnut, Indianapolis Hearings, December 17, 1991, at 11–12.

328   *Id.* at 30.

329   *See* Testimony of Chief Elizabeth Watson, Houston Police Department, HOUSTON HEARINGS, November 19, 1991, at 10 (testifying that "[i]t is not sufficient . . . to say that when we do that, things will be better."). *Id.*

330   *Id.* at 30. *See also* Testimony of Maj. Dennis R. Long, St. Louis County Police Department, ST. LOUIS HEARINGS, December 6, 1991, at 26; Testimony of Chief Clarence Harmon, St. Louis Metropolitan Police Department, ST. LOUIS HEARINGS, December 6, 1991, at 40 (testifying that the goal of the department has been to have 50% minorities in each recruit class, and that since before the 1990s about 47% of the class has been minorities); Testimony of Chief Kenneth Each, North Miami Beach Police Department, MIAMI HEARINGS, November 13, 1991, at 370–73 (testifying that he wants to bring the ratios of minorities within the police department up to those of the population).

331   *See* Testimony of Maj. Dennis R. Long, St. Louis County Police Department, ST. LOUIS HEARINGS, December 6, 1991, at 26.

332   *See, e.g.,* Testimony of Chief Charles Wall, Virginia Beach Police Department, NORFOLK HEARINGS, November 6, 1991, at 78; Testimony of Clarence Fisher, superintendent, Missouri State Highway Patrol, ST. LOUIS HEARINGS, December 6, 1991, at 18 (testifying that his department is in the process of revising its written affirmative action plan).

333   *See* Testimony of Maj. Dennis R. Long, St. Louis County Police Department, ST. LOUIS HEARINGS, December 6, 1991, at 26 (testifying that his department follows EEOC guidelines, but does not have a written affirmative action plan); Testimony of Chief Clarence Harmon, St. Louis Metropolitan Police Department, ST. LOUIS HEARINGS, December 6, 1991, at 56 (testifying that his department has a Special Issues Review Committee that reviews affirmative action issues in view of federal legislation, but does not have an affirmative action plan that would be approved by a federal agency and that identifies problems, establishes time tables, and is specifically monitored).

334   *See, e.g.,* Testimony of Chief Kenneth Each, North Miami Beach Police Department, MIAMI HEARINGS, November 13, 1991, at 370–73 (testifying that his department does not have an "accurate recruitment program" or affirmative action plan, and because of demographic growth the "ratios are way out," since the population of North Miami Beach is 43.6% white, 31.9% black, and 24.6% Hispanic, while the police department is 77% white, 6% black, and 15% Hispanic).

335   *See* Testimony of Clarence Fisher, superintendent, Missouri State Highway Patrol, ST. LOUIS HEARINGS, December 6, 1991, at 9.

336   *See* Testimony of Mayor Kathryn Whitmire, HOUSTON HEARINGS, November 19, 1991, at 17–18 (testifying that a proposal to allow the establishment of an affirmative action program in the police department was strongly endorsed by the Houston City Council, forty-four other city

councils, and the Texas Municipal League, but not adopted by the state legislature).

337 *See* Testimony of Mayor Xavier Suarez, MIAMI HEARINGS, November 12, 1991, at 72.

338 *See* Testimony of Chief Ian Shipley, Chesapeake Police Department, NORFOLK HEARINGS, November 6, 1991, at 73; Testimony of Maj. Sheldon Darden, chief of operations, Norfolk Police Department, NORFOLK HEARINGS, November 6, 1991, at 77; Testimony of Chief Charles Wall, Virginia Beach Police Department, NORFOLK HEARINGS, November 6, 1991, at 75–76; Testimony of Maj. Dennis R. Long, St. Louis County Police Department, ST. LOUIS HEARINGS, December 6, 1991, at 11. *See also* Testimony of Assistant Chief Hiram Contreras, Houston Police Department, HOUSTON HEARINGS, November 19, 1991, at 66 (testifying that his department targets local colleges for recruiting).

339 *See* Testimony of Chief Charles Wall, Virginia Beach Police Department, NORFOLK HEARINGS, November 6, 1991, at 75–76.

340 *See* Testimony of Chief Ian Shipley, Chesapeake Police Department, NORFOLK HEARINGS, November 6, 1991, at 73; Testimony of Maj. Sheldon Darden, chief of operations, Norfolk Police Department, NORFOLK HEARINGS, November 6, 1991, at 77.

341 *See* Testimony of Assistant Chief Hiram Contreras, Houston Police Department, HOUSTON HEARINGS, November 19, 1991, at 66, 80 (testifying that the Houston police consider themselves "a very military organization"). Recruitment of past or present military officers may be one way to increase the representation of minorities in police departments. However, caution should be exercised in recruiting those persons who might carry an "at war" mentality into community police work.

342 *See* Testimony of Deputy Chief Matthew Hunt, Los Angeles Police Department, LOS ANGELES HEARINGS, December 3, 1991, at 41; Testimony of Maj. Sheldon Darden, chief of operations, Norfolk Police Department, NORFOLK HEARINGS, November 6, 1991, at 77.

343 *See* Testimony of Deputy Chief Matthew Hunt, Los Angeles Police Department, LOS ANGELES HEARINGS, December 3, 1991, at 41.

344 *See* Testimony of Chief Ian Shipley, Chesapeake Police Department, NORFOLK HEARINGS, November 6, 1991, at 73.

345 *See* Testimony of Assistant Chief Hiram Contreras, Houston Police Department, HOUSTON HEARINGS, November 19, 1991, at 66–67. However, Rev. Jew Don Boney, National Black United Front, testified Houston spent $500,000 on a public relations effort to recruit minority police, of which $455,000 went to white firms. In one year Houston recruited 14 minorities. In 1991, up to the date of the hearings, of 159 recruits, 14 were black and 26 were Hispanic. *See* HOUSTON HEARINGS, November 19, 1991, at 389–94.

346 *See* Testimony of Chief Clarence Harmon, St. Louis Metropolitan

Police Department, Sᴛ. Lᴏᴜɪs Hᴇᴀʀɪɴɢs, December 6, 1991, at 40 (testifying that there were 20 African American students in the program).

347   *See* Testimony of Deputy Chief Matthew Hunt, Los Angeles Police Department, Lᴏs Aɴɢᴇʟᴇs Hᴇᴀʀɪɴɢs, December 3, 1991, at 41.

348   *See* Testimony of Maj. Sheldon Darden, chief of operations, Norfolk Police Department, Nᴏʀꜰᴏʟᴋ Hᴇᴀʀɪɴɢs, November 6, 1991, at 77.

349   *See* Testimony of Clarence Fisher, superintendent, Missouri State Highway Patrol, Sᴛ. Lᴏᴜɪs Hᴇᴀʀɪɴɢs, December 6, 1991, at 9.

350   *See* Testimony of Chief Calvin Ross, Miami Police Department, Mɪᴀᴍɪ Hᴇᴀʀɪɴɢs, November 13, 1991, at 461.

351   According to a 1992 survey of police departments in the 50 largest cities regarding the employment of black, Hispanic, and female officers, American police departments made only modest progress in employing African American and Hispanic police officers between 1982 and 1988, but made greater progress between 1988 and 1992. While a comparable survey found that only 10% of the cities had reached a hypothetical ideal level of employment (using an index comparing the percentage of a racial group in the police department against the percentage of that group in the local city population according to census figures) for both black and Hispanic officers in 1988, by 1992 38% of the police departments had reached the ideal level with respect to black officers. Twenty percent had reached the hypothetical ideal level for Hispanic officers, and none came close to the ideal level in employing women. The survey did not address the causes of progress or lack of progress in individual police departments. Sᴀᴍᴜᴇʟ Wᴀʟᴋᴇʀ & K B. ᴛᴜʀɴᴇʀ, A Dᴇᴄᴀᴅᴇ ᴏꜰ Mᴏᴅᴇsᴛ Pʀᴏɢʀᴇss (1992).

352   *See* Testimony of Chief Calvin Ross, Miami Police Department, Mɪᴀᴍɪ Hᴇᴀʀɪɴɢs, November 13, 1991, at 444 (testifying that in 1980 the composition of sworn personnel was 59% Anglo, 17% black, and 25% Hispanic, but is now 33% Anglo, 21% black, and 45% Hispanic, and that the current Miami population is 10% Anglo, 27% black, and 63% Hispanic). *See also* Fʟᴏʀɪᴅᴀ Aᴅᴠɪsᴏʀʏ Cᴏᴍᴍɪᴛᴛᴇᴇ ᴛᴏ ᴛʜᴇ Uɴɪᴛᴇᴅ Sᴛᴀᴛᴇs Cᴏᴍᴍɪssɪᴏɴ ᴏɴ Cɪᴠɪʟ Rɪɢʜᴛs, Pᴏʟɪᴄᴇ-Cᴏᴍᴍᴜɴɪᴛʏ Rᴇʟᴀᴛɪᴏɴs ɪɴ Mɪᴀᴍɪ (1989) (noting the improvement in the number of blacks and other minorities in the Miami and Metro-Dade Departments, the failure of the Florida Highway Patrol to comply with a court-ordered affirmative action plan, and complaints that the Florida Highway Patrol uses Dade County as a "dumping ground" for officers in need of disciplinary action).

See also Mɪᴀᴍɪ Pᴏʟɪᴄᴇ Dᴇᴘᴀʀᴛᴍᴇɴᴛ, 1990 Aɴɴᴜᴀʟ Rᴇᴘᴏʀᴛ, submitted at Mɪᴀᴍɪ Hᴇᴀʀɪɴɢs, November 12–13, 1991, at 25, giving the following demographic breakdown:

	% WHITE	% BLACK	% LATINO
Miami	10.1	27.4	62.5
Police Department (total)	28.7	30.4	40.4

sworn	34.0	20.7	44.7
civilian	15.8	53.7	30.1

Compare with 1992 report that 22.4% of the department is African American and 47.2% is Hispanic, while African Americans constitute 27.4% and Hispanics 61.5% of the Miami population. WALKER & TURNER, *supra* note 351.

353   *See* Testimony of Chief Calvin Ross, Miami Police Department, MIAMI HEARINGS, November 13, 1991, at 444.

354   *See* Sworn Work Force Comparison, 1980–1985–1991, submitted by Metro-Dade Police Department, MIAMI HEARINGS, November 12–13, 1991:

	% ANGLO	% BLACK	% HISPANIC
1980	84.2	8.1	7.7
1985	68.5	12.7	18.4
1991	57.7	15.4	26.6

See also FLORIDA ADVISORY COMMITTEE TO THE UNITED STATES COMMISSION ON CIVIL RIGHTS, POLICE-COMMUNITY RELATIONS IN MIAMI (1989).

355   *See* Testimony of Fred Taylor, director, Metro-Dade Police Department, MIAMI HEARINGS, November 12, 1991, at 87.

356   Research Division, Metro-Dade County Planning Department (citing 1990 census finding that 20.5% was African American, 49.2% was Hispanic, and 30.2% was Anglo).

357   WALKER & TURNER, *supra* note 351.

358   *See* Testimony of Chief Paul Anee, Indianapolis Police Department, INDIANAPOLIS HEARINGS, December 17, 1991, at 53. *See also* 1992 report that 17.8% of the Indianapolis Police Department in that year was African American, in contrast to 22.6% of the population of the city (1990 census figures). WALKER & TURNER, *supra* note 351.

359   *See* Testimony of Chief Charles Wall, Virginia Beach Police Department, NORFOLK HEARINGS, November 6, 1991, at 47, 78 (testifying that over the same period the percentage of women increased from 2% to 15%). *Compare with* 1992 report that 8.3% of the Virginia Beach Police Department is African American and 1.0% is Hispanic. WALKER & TURNER, *supra* note 351.

360   *See* Testimony of Clarence Fisher, superintendent, Missouri State Highway Patrol, ST. LOUIS HEARINGS, December 6, 1991, at 9 (testifying that 62 of the uninformed officers are African Americans and that there are 90 members of minority groups "wearing the blue uniform").

361   *Id.* at 18.

362   Testimony of Rev. Joseph Green, vice-mayor, City of Norfolk, NORFOLK HEARINGS, November 6, 1991, at 27.

363   *See* Testimony of Chief Ian Shipley, Chesapeake Police Department, Norfolk Hearings, November 6, 1991, at 36–37 (testifying that his
department had received an award within the last 3 years from the National Personnel Directors Association and support and compliments
from the local NAACP, and that there had been an increase of 3% in minority representation among sworn officers over the last year).

364   Testimony of Mayor William Ward, Chesapeake, Norfolk Hearings, November 6, 1991, at 99–100.

365   Testimony of Maj. Dennis R. Long, St. Louis County Police Department, St. Louis Hearings, December 6, 1991, at 11 (testifying that between October 1990 and October 1991, 20% of the applicants, and 32% of
those hired, were "minorities," consisting of six black men, three white
women, and one Hispanic man).

366   *Id.* at 11 (did not further define "minority").

367   *See* Testimony of Chief Clarence Harmon, St. Louis Metropolitan
Police Department, St. Louis Hearings, December 6, 1991, at 40 (testifying
that total minority representation, commissioned and civilian, is 32%, including 30% of the command staff).

368   *See* Testimony of Col. William H. Young, St. Louis Black Leadership Round Table, St. Louis Hearings, December 6, 1991, at 61. *See also*
Walker & Turner, *supra* note 351 (47.5% of St. Louis is African American,
compared to 28.2% of the police department).

369   *See* written materials from St. Louis Metropolitan Police Department, St. Louis Hearings, December 6, 1991.

370   *Id.*

371   Statement of Norman R. Seay, Legal Redress Chairperson, St.
Louis Branch, NAACP, St. Louis Hearings, December 6, 1991, at 56.

372   Similarly, Houston is 28% Hispanic, but this group makes up
only 12% of noncivilian personnel. *See* Testimony of Chief Elizabeth Watson, Houston Police Department, Houston Hearings, November 19, 1991,
at 31–32, 35. *Compare* with Walker & Turner, *supra* note 351 (finding that
African Americans constitute 28.1% and Hispanics 28.1% of the population of Houston [1990 census figures], while in 1992 14.7% of the police
department was African American and 12.5% Hispanic).

Houston has recently increased the educational requirements for
new hires. *See* Testimony of Mayor Kathryn Whitmire, Houston Hearings,
November 19, 1991, at 15. What effect the change will have on minority
representation in the police department remains to be seen.

373   Overall, noncivilian Houston police officers are 73% Anglo, 15%
black, 12% Hispanic, and 1% Asian. *See* Testimony of Chief Elizabeth Watson, Houston Police Department, Houston Hearings, November 19, 1991,
at 32.

374   *See* Testimony of Perry Wooten, chairman of the board, Afro
American Sheriffs Deputies League, Houston Hearings, November 19,
1991, at 235 ("In the Sheriff's Department . . . we have our own apartheid
here in Harris County."). They and the NAACP have filed a lawsuit challenging the sheriff's department for its hiring, promotions, disciplinary

actions, and racial harassment. In the sheriff's department, 18% of the 3,800 deputies are black; none of the administrative positions is held by a black or a Hispanic, and there is only one black captain. *Id.* at 238–39, 249.

375 Some officials described having greater flexibility in civilian appointments. *See, e.g.,* Testimony of Chief Elizabeth Watson, Houston Police Department, HOUSTON HEARINGS, November 19, 1991, at 31–32.

376 *See* Testimony of Chief Calvin Ross, Miami Police Department, MIAMI HEARINGS, November 13, 1991, at 444; Miami Police Department Personnel by Ethnicity and City of Miami Population by Ethnicity (based on 1990 census), MIAMI POLICE DEPARTMENT, 1990 ANNUAL REPORT, submitted by Miami Police Department, MIAMI HEARINGS, November 12–13, 1991.

377 *See* Testimony of Chief Lawrence L. Binkley, Long Beach Police Department, LOS ANGELES HEARINGS, December 4, 1991, at 67.

378 *See* Testimony of Chief Ian Shipley, Chesapeake Police Department, NORFOLK HEARINGS, November 6, 1991, at 37–38 (testifying that his department's efforts are reflected in a low turnover rate and advancement of minorities in supervisory positions).

379 *See* Testimony of Chief Elizabeth Watson, Houston Police Department, HOUSTON HEARINGS, November 19, 1991, at 31–32 (testifying that affirmative action for recruits and intermediate commanding officers is hamstrung by state law, which the city council and 44 others had tried unsuccessfully to get amended). *Id.* at 17–18. *See also* Testimony of Mayor Kathryn Whitmire, HOUSTON HEARINGS, November 19, 1991, at 30 ("Ethnic representation at the captain, lieutenant, and sergeant level is dismal.").

380 *See* Testimony of Justo Richard Garcia, president, Houston Police Organization of Spanish Speaking Officers, HOUSTON HEARINGS, November 20, 1991, at 9–10. *See also* Testimony of Chief Elizabeth Watson, Houston Police Department, HOUSTON HEARINGS, November 19, 1991, at 32 (testifying that 12% of Houston police officers are Hispanic and 15% are African American).

381 *See* November 19, 1991, letter to Keryl Smith, Houston NAACP, from Michael O. Adams, Ph.D., associate professor, Administration of Justice Program, Texas Southern University, written submission at HOUSTON HEARINGS, November 19–20, 1991 (citing Houston Police Department personnel data in November 1991 Coins Report).

382 *See* Testimony of Col. William H. Young, St. Louis Black Leadership Round Table, ST. LOUIS HEARINGS, December 6, 1991, at 61.

383 WALKER & TURNER, *supra* note 351 (reporting that, according to the 1990 census, 13.9% of the population of Virginia Beach was African American).

384 *See* Metro-Dade Police Department Workforce Analyses, submitted by Metro-Dade Police Department, MIAMI HEARINGS, November 12–13, 1991. Of the sworn force, 12.3% is Hispanic. *Id.*

385 *See* Testimony of Fred Taylor, director, Metro-Dade Police De-

partment, MIAMI HEARINGS, November 12, 1991, at 118 (testifying that he is pleased with the racial composition and change over the last decade in the rank of initial supervisors and in the appointed positions—he and the county manager appointed the top sixty positions—and that the weakness, if any, is in the middle-management jobs). *See also* Sworn Work Force Comparison and Metro-Dade Police Department Workforce Analyses, submitted by Metro-Dade Police Department at MIAMI HEARINGS, November 12–13, 1991.

386   WALKER & TURNER, *supra* note 351.

387   Testimony of Odell McGawan, ST. LOUIS HEARINGS, December 6, 1991, at 33. *See also* Testimony of Maj. Dennis R. Long, St. Louis County Police Department, ST. LOUIS HEARINGS, December 6, 1991, at 12 (testifying that currently 18% of all minority officers hold supervisory or command positions in his department).

388   *See* Testimony of Chief Clarence Harmon, St. Louis Metropolitan Police Department, ST. LOUIS HEARINGS, December 6, 1991, at 40 (testifying that he is the department's first African American chief and that he had been chief for four months at the time of the Miami hearings).

389   *See* Finding F5, *supra* 84–90.

390   WALKER & TURNER, *supra* note 351.

391   Testimony of Deloyd Parker, executive director, SHAPE (Self Help for African People through Education), HOUSTON HEARINGS, November 19, 1991, at 256–57.

392   Testimony of Chief Elizabeth Watson, Houston Police Department, HOUSTON HEARINGS, November 19, 1991, at 35 ("[T]he officers themselves criticize [the promotional system] as a multiple choice exam that is memory-driven.").

393   Testimony of Mayor Kathryn Whitmire, HOUSTON HEARINGS, November 19, 1991, at 31.

394   *Id.* at 17–18.

395   *Id.* at 18.

396   *Id.* at 32 (testifying they are not restricted by state law in their management of civilian personnel).

397   *See* Testimony of Chief Elizabeth Watson, Houston Police Department, HOUSTON HEARINGS, November 19, 1991, at 33.

398   *See* Testimony of Rev. Jew Don Boney, National Black United Front, HOUSTON HEARINGS, November 20, 1991, at 389–94.

399   *See* Testimony of Maj. Dennis R. Long, St. Louis County Police Department, ST. LOUIS HEARINGS, December 6, 1991, at 29.

400   *See* Testimony of Col. William H. Young, St. Louis Black Leadership Round Table, ST. LOUIS HEARINGS, December 6, 1991, at 68.

401   *See* Testimony of Maj. Dennis R. Long, St. Louis County Police Department, ST. LOUIS HEARINGS, December 6, 1991, at 11 (testifying that the degree requirement is waived if the officer has five years' experience in the next lower rank).

402   *See id.* at 11.

403   Testimony of Mayor Kathryn Whitmire, HOUSTON HEARINGS, November 19, 1991, at 15 (expressing pride in the diversity of these levels, testified that of 11 assistant chiefs appointed by the chief and confirmed by the city council, 2 are Hispanic, 2 are African American, and 1 is a woman). *Id.* at 30.

404   Testimony of Fred Taylor, director, Metro-Dade Police Department, MIAMI HEARINGS, November 12, 1991, at 118.

405   *See* Testimony of Chief Ian Shipley, Chesapeake Police Department, NORFOLK HEARINGS, November 6, 1991, at 37–38.

406   Testimony of Maj. Sheldon Darden, chief of operations, Norfolk Police Department, NORFOLK HEARINGS, November 6, 1991, at 87 (also testified that when he achieved the rank of captain, a reverse discrimination complaint was filed). *Id.*

407   *See id.*

408   *See, e.g.,* Testimony of Mayor William Hudnut, INDIANAPOLIS HEARINGS, December 17, 1991, at 12; Testimony of David Shaheed, president-elect, Marion County Bar Association, INDIANAPOLIS HEARINGS, December 17, 1991, at 135 (advocating continued training, including sensitivity training, of police officers despite their length of service on the force); Testimony of Doug Elder, president, Houston Police Officers Association, HOUSTON HEARINGS, November 20, 1991, at 66 (testifying that his organization supported proposed legislation to make cultural-diversity and sensitivity training mandatory for all police officers in Texas); Testimony of Helen Gros, executive director, Texas ACLU, HOUSTON HEARINGS, November 19, 1991, at 159 ("Officers must be trained not only in the essentials of law enforcement and Criminal Justice, but also in interpersonal relations."); Testimony of Deloyd Parker, executive director, SHAPE, HOUSTON HEARINGS, November 19, 1991, at 266 (testifying that officers presently on the force and on the streets should go back for further training in cultural differences); Testimony of Liz Morris, education coordinator, Houston Area Women's Center, HOUSTON HEARINGS, November 20, 1991, at 80 (testifying that the report of their family-violence unit recommended mandatory training for all levels in the police department to eliminate sexist, racist, and homophobic behaviors, as well as increasing the number of female officers); Testimony of Mayor Xavier Suarez, MIAMI HEARINGS, November 12, 1991, at 50, 74 (testifying that his recommendations to the city manager and police chief for sensitivity programs, for officers to live in the area, and to go into the community in nonprofessional settings has not been well received because of bureaucracy).

409   Testimony of Mary Redd, Urban League, NORFOLK HEARINGS, November 6, 1991, at 156.

410   Testimony of Mayor Xavier Suarez, MIAMI HEARINGS, November 12, 1991, at 50, 74.

411   *See, e.g.,* Testimony of Chief Charles Wall, Virginia Beach Police Department, Norfolk Hearings, November 6, 1991, at 58.

412   *See* Testimony of Maj. Dennis Long, St. Louis County Police Department, St. Louis Hearings, December 6, 1991, at 23.

413   *See* Testimony of Chief Clarence Harmon, St. Louis Metropolitan Police Department, St. Louis Hearings, December 6, 1991, at 41.

414   *See* Testimony of Clarence Fisher, superintendent, Missouri State Highway Patrol, St. Louis Hearings, December 6, 1991, at 8, 23.

415   *See* Testimony of Chief Calvin Ross, Miami Police Department, Miami Hearings, November 13, 1991, at 469.

416   *See* Testimony of Fred Taylor, director, Metro-Dade Police Department, Miami Hearings, November 12, 1991, at 88.

417   *See* Testimony of Deputy Chief Matthew Hunt, Los Angeles Police Department, Los Angeles Hearings, December 3, 1991, at 38.

418   *Id.* at 53.

419   *See* Testimony of Assistant Chief Hiram Contreras, Houston Police Department, Houston Hearings, November 19, 1991, at 70–72.

420   *See* Testimony of Chief Elizabeth Watson, Houston Police Department, Houston Hearings, November 19, 1991, at 10–11.

421   Twenty percent responded to a questionnaire sent to all 5,500 employees of the Houston Police Department (77% male, 67% white, 19% black, 8% Hispanic, 2% Asian; 70% officers, 25% civilians). Between one-third and one-half reported that they had experienced sex or race discrimination and did nothing about it due to fear of retaliation. Sixty-four percent felt that race discrimination was present in the department, and 42% felt that there was sex discrimination in the department. Significantly, 72.5% felt that affirmative action resulted in reverse discrimination. *See* Final Report of the Houston Police Department Survey: Perceptions of Discrimination and of the Grievance Procedures, July 31, 1991, prepared by Vicki A. Lucas, University of Texas, submitted at Houston Hearings, November 19–20, 1991.

422   *See* Testimony of Chief Calvin Ross, Miami Police Department, Miami Hearings, November 13, 1991, at 469.

423   Testimony of Justo Garcia, Houston Hearings, November 20, 1991, at 12–13.

424   *See, e.g.,* Testimony of Maj. Dennis R. Long, St. Louis County Police Department, St. Louis Hearings, December 6, 1991, at 23 (testifying that his department has annual in-service training on cultural-awareness issues, but did not specify the amount of training or who was required to participate in it); Testimony of Chief Charles Wall, Virginia Beach Police Department, Norfolk Hearings, November 6, 1991, at 58 (testifying that his department provides training in "cultural awareness," managing conflicts to reduce conflicts, and "verbal judo" as the first level of force, but did not specify the amount or frequency of this training).

425   *See* Testimony of Chief Calvin Ross, Miami Police Department, MIAMI HEARINGS, November 13, 1991, at 445.

426   *Id.* at 445.

427   *Id.* at 446, and written materials submitted by the Miami Police Department.

428   *Id.* at 446 (testifying that the department spent $35,000 to support the training and had sponsored community representatives, students, and ten police officers in this program).

429   *Id.* at 446–47.

430   *See* Testimony of Fred Taylor, director, Metro-Dade Police Department, MIAMI HEARINGS, November 12, 1991, at 88, and written materials submitted by his department. Except as specified, and pursuant to information that all sworn officers in 1988 and 1989 were required to participate in violence-reduction training, the number of officers taking part in these programs, how often, and whether the training is required or voluntary was not specified.

431   *See* Testimony of Assistant Chief Hiram Contreras, Houston Police Department, HOUSTON HEARINGS, November 19, 1991, at 71.

432   *See* Testimony of Chief Clarence Harmon, St. Louis Metropolitan Police Department, ST. LOUIS HEARINGS, December 6, 1991, at 41.

433   *See, e.g.,* Testimony of Fred Taylor, director, Metro-Dade Police Department, MIAMI HEARINGS, November 12, 1991, at 122; Testimony of Chief Jimmy R. Burke, Opa-Locka Police Department, MIAMI HEARINGS, November 12, 1991, at 122.

434   *See* Testimony of Mayor William Ward, Chesapeake, NORFOLK HEARINGS, November 6, 1991, at 117.

435   *See* Testimony of Chief Elizabeth Watson, Houston Police Department, HOUSTON HEARINGS, November 19, 1991, at 39.

436   *See, e.g.,* Testimony of Ada Edwards, HOUSTON HEARINGS, November 19, 1991, at 438 (criticizing the Houston "sensitivity training" as not having been designed with community input).

437   *See* Testimony of Chief Calvin Ross, Miami Police Department, MIAMI HEARINGS, November 13, 1991, at 446–47.

438   *See* written materials provided by the Miami Police Department.

439   Testimony of Shelby Lanier, chairman, National Black Police Association, INDIANAPOLIS HEARINGS, December 17, 1991, at 272–73. Lanier also testified that the National Black Police Association has more than 35,000 members and over 125 chapters in 33 states and the District of Columbia. *Id.* at 270–71.

440   *See* CHRISTOPHER COMMISSION REPORT, at 69.

441   Almost all of those interviewed by the Christopher Commission described the regularity of racially derogatory remarks at roll call and the frequent posting of racist jokes and cartoons on bulletin boards and in locker rooms. Most, however, put up with such conduct to avoid being labeled sensitive or thin-skinned. *See* CHRISTOPHER COMMISSION REPORT, at

79–80. The report also summarizes a 1987 survey in which 45% of the African American officers, 31% of the Latino officers, and 25% of the Asian officers said they had encountered race discrimination; 45% of African American male officers, 27% of Latino male officers, and 31% of Asian male officers had experienced racial slurs by supervisors, peers, or both, while the percentages of females with such experiences were 40% for African Americans, 36% for Latinos, and 24% for Asians. *See id.* at 81.

442   Witnesses before the Christopher Commission contrasted the strong response of the Los Angeles Police Department to narcotic use, theft, and other criminal acts by officers with the failure to enforce policies against racial and ethnic bias. *See* CHRISTOPHER COMMISSION REPORT, at 79.

443   *Id.*

444   Testimony of John Mack, Urban League, LOS ANGELES HEARINGS, December 3, 1991, at 39. *See also* Testimony of Don Stephenson, LOS ANGELES HEARINGS, December 3, 1991, at 125 ("The attitude of the community towards the police varies. The elderly and the homeowners are fearful of crime and drugs and frequently willing to accept the occasional police abuse for protection. The underclass are preyed upon by the criminals and the police. Therefore, they see no distinction between them.").

445   *See, e.g.,* Testimony of Rev. Willie Simms, Metro-Dade Community Affairs, Black Affairs Program, MIAMI HEARINGS, November 12, 1991, at 67.

446   Testimony of Dr. Helen Green, NORFOLK HEARINGS, November 6, 1991, at 16, 17.

447   Testimony of Rickie Clark, National Black Police Association, INDIANAPOLIS HEARINGS, December 17, 1991, at 260.

448   Testimony of Herman E. Springs, director of police, Norfolk State University, NORFOLK HEARINGS, November 6, 1991, at 23.

449   *See, e.g.,* Testimony of Jeanette Amadeo, MIAMI HEARINGS, November 13, 1991, at 701.

450   Testimony of Deborah Gordon, MIAMI HEARINGS, November 13, 1991, at 701.

451   Testimony of Wanda Gonzalez, MIAMI HEARINGS, November 12, 1991, at 305.

452   *Id.* at 308–10.

453   Testimony of Chief Ian Shipley, Chesapeake Police Department, NORFOLK HEARINGS, November 6, 1991, at 45. *See also* CHRISTOPHER COMMISSION REPORT, at 69 (stating that of the 650 officers who responded to their survey on police and the community, almost two-thirds agreed that increased interaction with the community would improve police-community relations).

454   *See* Testimony of Herman E. Springs, director of police, Norfolk State University, NORFOLK HEARINGS, November 6, 1991, at 26.

455   *Id.* at 27, 29.

456   Testimony of Mafundi Jitahadi, Los Angeles Hearings, December 3, 1991, at 96.

457   Testimony of Shelby Lanier, chairman, National Black Police Association, Indianapolis Hearings, December 17, 1991, at 272–73.

458   Testimony of Deputy Chief Matthew Hunt, Los Angeles Police Department, Los Angeles Hearings, December 3, 1991, at 46.

459   *Id.*

Notes to Recommendations for Change

1   One need only recall Sergeant Jablonski on television's "Hill Street Blues," who ended each morning roll call with the rallying cry, "Let's do it to them before they do it to us." Though television is not always an accurate reflection of real life, "those words surely express an insider/outsider vision typical of traditional police culture." Jerome Skolnick & David H. Bayley, The New Blue Line 211 (1986).

2   *See, e.g.,* Testimony of Ernie Neal, vice-president, Miami chapter of NOBLE, Miami Hearings, November 13, 1991, at 582–84 (testifying that police officers are set apart from the rest of urban society by their tendency to socialize only with each other, by contempt for civilians, and by their migration outside of urban areas); Testimony of Dr. Larry Capp, psychologist, Miami Hearings, November 12, 1991, at 259 ("Unfortunately it is quite common for police officers to reside in other communities or even outside the county but only come into the city to go to work."); Testimony of Testimony of Chief Calvin Ross, Miami Police Department, Miami Hearings, November 12, 1991, at 443 ("There has been a traditional sense in both law enforcement and the general public as a community composed of two cultures, the served and the servers or more specifically, they enforce [*sic*] and those upon whom the law is enforced. . . . [If] this notion is allowed to flourish [it] will polarize our community, will undermine any progress. . . .").

3   *See, e.g.,* Testimony of Marvin Jones, University of Miami School of Law, Miami Hearings, November 12, 1991, at 185–86 (referring to a sociological study of police misconduct in another city which found that the police identified with residents in white communities but not in black communities, referring to the latter as "them"); Testimony of Ernie Neal, vice-president, Miami chapter of NOBLE, Miami Hearings, November 13, 1991, at 582 ("As a result of the increased isolation of policemen from civilians because of the spread of the radio car and the demographic changes in cities, policemen have become more contemptuous than ever of civilians."). *See also* Anthony V. Bouza, The Police Mystique 6 ("The mystery begins with the fabled insularity of the police. It is not an accident that cops speak of the 'outside world' and of 'civilians' with a barely concealed scorn for the uninitiated. The fact that they think of their pre-

cincts as embattled fortresses in alien lands reflects, at once, their problems with the minorities they've been sent to police and their resentment toward an overclass that has issued the sub rosa marching orders.'").

4   *See, e.g.,* Testimony of Ernie Neal, vice-president, Miami chapter of NOBLE, MIAMI HEARINGS, November 13, 1991, at 582 ("Many police [officers] come to believe that no matter how respectable the facade, most men and women are still animals underneath and that it does not take much for the veneer to be stripped away and the reality underneath to show through.").

5   *See* Testimony of Chief Calvin Ross, Miami Police Department, MIAMI HEARINGS, November 13, 1991, at 454 ("[T]he process . . . is not one that is going to be an overnight change.").

6   *See* Testimony of Chief Lawrence L. Binkley, Long Beach Police Department, LOS ANGELES HEARINGS, December 4, 1991, at 69 ("I think there are a lot of Chiefs who would like to change organizations but find very little support. . . . When you change an organization's culture, which requires the termination of employees and very tough discipline, there are police unions who are very strong politically and have a great deal of money and get involved in politics that do not want those changes. When a chief from anywhere in the nation tries to change a culture, he is taken on vigorously, and I see very few allies when he does that to support his changes.").

7   *See* Testimony of Chief Calvin Ross, Miami Police Department, MIAMI HEARINGS, November 13, 1991, at 462–63 ("[O]ne of the things we are trying to overcome today . . . is . . . the perception by different minority groups within our community of the police and some of these old perceptions and mind sets are hard to deal with, and they are hard to overcome. . . . We are trying to give the community a different view of the police department . . . to let them know that law enforcement is an honorable profession and one that . . . [they] would do well to join the ranks of."); Testimony of Ernie Neal, vice-president, Miami chapter of NOBLE, MIAMI HEARINGS, November 13, 1991, at 584–85 (". . . African American cities can be safe only if they become true communities where all of the people see themselves as engaged in a common enterprise and share a common fate. . . . [I]f we do not make the attempt, we may be doomed to ever-increasing hostility, violence and despair."); Testimony of Deputy Chief Matthew Hunt, Los Angeles Police Department, LOS ANGELES HEARINGS, December 3, 1991, at 46.

8   *See* Testimony of Mayor Xavier Suarez, MIAMI HEARINGS, November 12, 1991, at 50 ("[O]fficers who patrol a certain area should understand that area and . . . at least figure out a way to do it in a nonprofessional setting with the people."); Testimony of Dr. Larry Capp, psychologist, MIAMI HEARINGS, November 12, 1991, at 259–60 (testifying that research indicates that when officers are more a part of the "fabric of the

community by having an investment there, residing there . . . [i]t leads to a better situation all around.'').

9   *See, e.g.,* Testimony of Dr. Larry Capp, psychologist, MIAMI HEARINGS, November 12, 1991, at 258–59 (testifying that research in police science supports the idea that having officers who know, live, and have families in the area results in better policing because of their knowledge of the community and their sense of ownership and commitment).

10   Testimony of Sylvia Brooks, president, Houston Urban League, HOUSTON HEARINGS, November 19, 1991, at 205–6.

11   *See, e.g.,* Testimony of Rev. James Taylor, Indiana Interreligious Commission on Human Rights Equality, INDIANAPOLIS HEARINGS, December 17, 1991, at 157; Testimony of Deloyd Parker, executive director, SHAPE, HOUSTON HEARINGS, November 19, 1991, at 266–67; Testimony of Kathleen Worthy, UP-PAC, MIAMI HEARINGS, November 13, 1991, at 485 (testifying that police officers and firefighters should be required to live in the community "so that their off-duty conduct and associations can be monitored"). *See also* MALCOLM K. SPARROW ET AL., BEYOND 911, at 34 (1990) (". . . [T]he early American . . . police forces had certain strengths. One of the foremost was that—drawn from and operating from within their communities—they enjoyed a fair degree of local support and political legitimacy. Officers usually lived in or close to the areas they patrolled."); ROBERT M. FOGELSON, BIG-CITY POLICE 289 (1977) ("[In the early 1970s,] [m]any Americans also called on the authorities to reimpose the residency requirements, a move, they argued, that would not only increase the competitive edge of the blacks and other minorities but also improve the quality of law enforcement and alleviate the fiscal crisis of the cities. But the rank-and-file outfits strongly objected to this proposal. Stressing that it would violate the civil liberties of the officers and, by excluding qualified candidates from out of town and compelling veteran officers to choose between their jobs and their homes, lower the caliber of the police departments, they opposed it in one city after another."). *But see* Testimony of Mayor Xavier Suarez, MIAMI HEARINGS, November 12, 1991, at 74 (testifying that the proposal for police officers to live in housing projects, with rent subsidies, was approved but never implemented); *Boston Officer Backs Bias Call,* BOSTON GLOBE, Aug. 3, 1992, at 13–14 (The president of the Massachusetts Association of Minority Law Enforcement Officers says the Boston Police Department maintains a "double standard" and disciplines minority officers more harshly than white officers. "You get the feeling you can't be trusted because a lot of minority officers live in the communities that they police and there's a lot of crimes in those communities. . . ."); *Ex-Officer Says Roots in Community Cost Him His Job,* BOSTON GLOBE, Aug. 4, 1992, at 13, 16 ("Questions arise sometimes in the minds of white officers about minority officers based on who they grew up with or where they live—things that may have no relevance to their ability to do the job. . . .").

12   See, e.g., Testimony of Chief Clarence Harmon, St. Louis Metropolitan Police Department, St. Louis Hearings, December 6, 1991, at 49 (testifying that officers appointed after 1973 must become residents of St. Louis within 90 days of their appointment); Testimony of Dr. Larry Capp, psychologist, Miami Hearings, November 12, 1991, at 259 (testifying that many cities now have residency requirements for new recruits and that some departments are experimenting with giving incentives, such as free apartments, to induce officers to live where they work).

13   See, e.g., Testimony of Janet Reno, Dade County state's attorney, Miami Hearings, November 12, 1991, at 17 (testifying that police officers should be "known in the community and work in the community").

14   See, e.g., Testimony of Chief Calvin Ross, Miami Police Department, Miami Hearings, November 13, 1991, at 464–65 ("[W]e have officers that are volunteering to be involved in [community] . . . programs . . . other than just . . . in the enforcement mode. . . . [P]olice actually go out and have picnics in different communities in the parks with the youth. . . . We have police officers . . . involving themselves with community forums.").

15   See, e.g., Testimony of Chief Calvin Ross, Miami Police Department, Miami Hearings, November 13, 1991, at 464–65 ("[O]ur police officers are being seen in . . . [community] forums as being a part of the community and do not necessarily act as law enforcers, but as social workers, if you will, and as problem solvers.").

16   See Skolnick & Bayley, supra note 1, at 211 ("The typical police department is paramilitary, regulated by the civil service, unionized, and opposed to lateral entry."). See also Fogelson, supra note 11, at 40–66.

17   See, e.g., Sparrow et al., supra note 11, at 34 (". . . [T]he early American . . . police forces simply assumed responsibility for whatever emergencies and crises crossed their paths. On the principle that if it needed to be done, and nobody was doing it, they would, various forces provided ambulance services, ran soup kitchens, collected garbage, and sheltered homeless. . . . In a time before widespread and well-supported social work and social programs, and before municipalities had assumed many of their current routine obligations, the police often filled important vacuums.").

18   See Herman Goldstein, Policing a Free Society 24–28 (1977) (". . . [R]ecent studies of the police have dwelled on the high percentage of police time spent on other than criminal matters, and they thus call into question the value of viewing the police primarily as a part of the criminal justice system. . . . The studies report the large number of hours devoted to handling accidents and illness, stray and injured animals, and intoxicated persons; dealing with family disturbances, fights among teen-age gangs, and noisy gatherings; taking reports on damage to property, traffic accidents, missing persons, and lost and found property. They cite the

amount of time devoted to administering systems of registration and licensing; to directing traffic; to dealing with complaints of improper parking; to controlling crowds at public events; and to dealing with numerous hazards and municipal service defects that require attention.").

19   *See id.* at 25.

20   *See id.*

21   *See* Mark H. Moore ET AL., *Crime and Policing,* PERSPECTIVES ON POLICING, no. 2 (National Institute of Justice and Harvard University, 1988).

22   *See* Testimony of Chief Jerry Oliver, Pasadena Police Department, LOS ANGELES HEARINGS, December 4, 1991, at 119 (describing changes in his department, Oliver testified: "We brought what we consider to be a corporateness to a public sector industry . . . and we expect to return a dividend . . . not just of providing . . . 'law enforcement services' . . . but a dividend of providing an array of police services that includes law enforcement. . . . [T]he other parts . . . deal more proactively with prevention . . . and the operation . . . will have most of its resources and . . . energies going towards prevention, that is, being even more involved in education and in the development of healthy human beings within the . . . community."). *See also* James Q. Wilson & George L. Kelling, *Broken Windows,* ATLANTIC MONTHLY, March 1982, at 29 (arguing that police attention to signs of disorder in a neighborhood may be more important than attention to violent crime).

23   GOLDSTEIN, *supra* note 18, at 25.

24   *See, e.g.,* Testimony of Janet Reno, Dade County state's attorney, MIAMI HEARINGS, November 12, 1991, at 17–18 (testifying that "to overcome a history of economic, social and racial injustice" there should be a team approach that goes beyond team policing to identifying and "carving out small enough neighborhoods" to enable a "return to one-on-one contact," and that the team should include a public health nurse, a social worker, and a "community respected police officer" assigned as a team with a 5-year commitment to that neighborhood); Testimony of Councilperson Mark Ridley-Thomas, LOS ANGELES HEARINGS, December 3, 1991, at 15 ("The goal of policing is to protect and serve and improve the quality of life for the citizens. . . . The effect is collaborative problem-solving between the community and the police department. And the key components would be active policing and involvement and innovative police work. The idea that . . . the business of law enforcement and fighting crime is solely the domain of the police . . . is virtually nonsensical. The police department cannot handle the range of problems that need to be addressed.").

25   *See* Testimony of Chief Calvin Ross, Miami Police Department, MIAMI HEARINGS, November 13, 1991, at 466–67 ("[T]hroughout our government we have for the most part pretty much of a Band-Aid solution [to] . . . a lot of the problems that exist in the community as it relates to

police and citizens in problems with drugs and crime. If we had . . . [placed a lot of emphasis on projects and programs toward young people] ten years ago, we would be . . . much further along. . . . I believe we must start to target tomorrow.").

26 *See, e.g.*, Testimony of Johnny Mata, League of United Latin American Citizens, HOUSTON HEARINGS, November 19, 1991, at 164; Testimony of Doug Elder, president, Houston Police Officers Association, HOUSTON HEARINGS, November 19, 1991, at 35 (testifying that due to Houston's financial problems over the last decade, "the average veteran officer has lost 22% of their [*sic*] buying power which has created a strain. . . .").

27 REPORT OF THE INDEPENDENT COMMISSION ON THE LOS ANGELES POLICE DEPARTMENT (1991) [hereinafter CHRISTOPHER COMMISSION REPORT], at 170.

28 *Id.* at iii.

29 *See* Testimony of Troy Smith, Greater Watts Justice Center, LOS ANGELES HEARINGS, December 3, 1991, at 89 ("What is most troubling is that much of the physical violence and suffering inflicted by many public officers are dismissed or justified by many public officials as the result of an increase in violent crime. It is very true that the residents of poor and minority communities desire and need police protection but certainly not at the expense of their civil rights or, in some cases, their li[ves]. A close review of the complaints filed with my office reveals that a large majority of physical and verbal altercations involving police officers were with individuals in custody, under controlled situations of no danger to the officer."); Testimony of John Mack, Urban League, LOS ANGELES HEARINGS, December 3, 1991, at 39 ("[W]e have the situation where police departments such as the LAPD have been given free license to disregard peoples' civil liberties within the problem of going after the gangs and the drugs, and people turn their heads the other way.").

30 CHRISTOPHER COMMISSION REPORT, at 228.

31 *See* Testimony of Chief Michael McCrary, Signal Hill Police Department, LOS ANGELES HEARINGS, December 4, 1991, at 123 ("I met with all employees . . . sworn and non-sworn . . . and discussed role expectations. I told them what they could expect from me. What the expectations were of them, and what the consequences were if they violated those expectations. I felt that was very important for the trust level, that they knew exactly where I was coming from, what my mission was, what my standards were, and what my values were. Very important that the employees understand that from the head of the department.").

32 REPORT OF THE BOSTON POLICE DEPARTMENT MANAGEMENT REVIEW COMMISSION (1992) [hereinafter ST. CLAIR COMMISSION REPORT], at 52.

33 *See id.* at 61–62. *See also* Testimony of Minga Wigfall, MIAMI HEARINGS, November 13, 1991, at 571 (testifying that pressures on officers can be "minimized or eliminated entirely by following appropriate code of conduct regulations with effective guidelines concerning police discretion").

34 CHRISTOPHER COMMISSION REPORT, at 174.

35 Geoffrey P. Alpert & Mark H. Moore, "Measuring Police Performance in the New Paradigm of Policing," *Performance Measures for the Criminal Justice System* 109 (Discussion Papers from the Bureau of Justice Statistics–Princeton University Study Group on Criminal Justice, October 1993).

36 *Id.* at 111.

37 *Id.* at 113.

38 *See id.* at 123.

39 *Id.* at 113–14, 126–30.

40 *See, e.g.,* Testimony of David Honig, general counsel, Miami-Dade Branch, NAACP, MIAMI HEARINGS, November 12, 1991, at 178–79 (testifying that incentives for reporting misconduct by a fellow officer should be "counterbalanced by positive incentives for pro-social behavior").

41 *See* CHRISTOPHER COMMISSION REPORT, at 142, 148.

42 ST. CLAIR COMMISSION REPORT, at 63.

43 *See, e.g.,* Testimony of Fred Taylor, director, Metro-Dade Police Department, MIAMI HEARINGS, November 12, 1991, at 88 ("[T]o make sure that we don't encounter the kind of things you saw out in Los Angeles . . . [i]t takes hard work and commitment to hire trained supervisors . . . [and supervisors must be] required to take direct action against those who don't follow . . . rules and . . . policies. . . .").

44 *Id.* at 70.

45 *Id. See also* Testimony of Chief Elizabeth Watson, Houston Police Department, HOUSTON HEARINGS, November 19, 1991, at 47 (testifying that surveys are being developed); Testimony of Assistant Chief Phyllis Wunsche, Houston Police Department, IAD, HOUSTON HEARINGS, November 19, 1991, at 65 (testifying that community groups will be invited to make recommendations for commendations).

46 *See* CHRISTOPHER COMMISSION REPORT, at 175, for a description of such a system. *See also* Testimony of Chief Elizabeth Watson, Houston Police Department, HOUSTON HEARINGS, November 19, 1991, at 8; Testimony of Assistant Chief Phyllis Wunsche, Houston Police Department, IAD, HOUSTON HEARINGS, November 19, 1991, at 99–102, 112; Testimony of Assistant Chief Jimmy L. Dotson, Houston Police Department, HOUSTON HEARINGS, November 19, 1991, at 132–35.

47 *See* CHRISTOPHER COMMISSION REPORT, at 175.

48 *Id. See also* Testimony of Assistant Chief Phyllis Wunsche, Houston Police Department, IAD, HOUSTON HEARINGS, November 19, 1991, at 99.

49 *See* CHRISTOPHER COMMISSION REPORT, chapter 10. *See also* Testimony of Dr. Larry Capp, psychologist, MIAMI HEARINGS, November 12, 1991, at 235 (testifying that police departments are paramilitary in nature, responding to a chain of command, and that the chief "sets the tone for

[the] entire department" and "has to show a great deal of leadership . . . and strength in setting the tone for how he wants his officers to behave").

50 *See, e.g.,* Testimony of David Honig, general counsel, Miami-Dade Branch, NAACP, MIAMI HEARINGS, November 12, 1991, at 177 ("[P]eople who have the ultimate responsibility for police misconduct, mayors and police chiefs, need to, individually and collectively, make a statement of police procedures which, in some cases but not all, would be simply a reiteration of procedures which are on the books but seldom enforced. That is, in order to enhance public confidence.").

51 *See, e.g.,* Testimony of Chief Elizabeth Watson, Houston Police Department, HOUSTON HEARINGS, November 19, 1991, at 35; Testimony of Mayor Kathryn Whitmire, HOUSTON HEARINGS, November 19, 1991, at 17.

52 For an example of the controversy over civil service in this context, *compare* Testimony of Chief Elizabeth Watson, Houston Police Department, HOUSTON HEARINGS, November 19, 1991, at 35 *with* Testimony of Doug Elder, president, Houston Police Officers Association, HOUSTON HEARINGS, November 20, 1991, at 20–21, 49.

53 *See, e.g.,* Testimony of James Beauford, Urban League, Metropolitan St. Louis, ST. LOUIS HEARINGS, December 6, 1991, at 36 (his recommendations for police departments include: development, publication, and distribution of the department's affirmative action plan; an increase in the percentage of African American officers and African American officers in command-rank positions to a percentage commensurate with the African American population in St. Louis; an increase in the percentage of African American officers in specialized units and receiving specialized training); Testimony of Sanders Anderson, Department of Public Affairs, Texas Southern University, HOUSTON HEARINGS, November 19, 1991, at 297; Testimony of Fred Taylor, director, Metro-Dade Police Department, MIAMI HEARINGS, November 12, 1991, at 87 ("I firmly believe that if you are going to police the community . . . you have to look like the community."); Testimony of Msgr. Brian Walsh, Catholic Commission for Social Advocacies, MIAMI HEARINGS, November 12, 1991, at 191 ("[T]he police force should be representative of the entire community and all its levels."); Testimony of Clemente Montalvo, MIAMI HEARINGS, November 12, 1991, at 324 (recommending increase in Puerto Rican officers patrolling Puerto Rican neighborhoods); Testimony of John Pace, MIAMI HEARINGS, November 13, 1991, at 717 (recommending more minorities in the police department structure); Alexander Cockburn, *Beat the Devil,* NATION, June 1, 1992, at 738–39 (reporting that the " 'Bloods/Crips Proposal for L.A.'s Facelift' " includes a demand that communities be " 'policed and patrolled by individuals who live in the community.' "). *See also* "WHERE THE INJURED FLY FOR JUSTICE," REPORT AND RECOMMENDATIONS OF THE FLORIDA SUPREME COURT RACIAL AND ETHNIC BIAS STUDY COMMISSION (1990) [hereinafter "WHERE THE INJURED FLY FOR JUSTICE" (recommending that law-enforcement agencies adopt plans to recruit, hire, retain, and promote minorities and create a

minority career-development program); OFFICE OF PROFESSIONAL COMPLI-
ANCE, REPORT ON THE HAITIAN DISTURBANCE, JUNE 29–JULY 7, 1990 (referring to
a 1980 study by the National Minority Advisory Council on Criminal Justice that found that the presence of minority officers has had a positive
effect on police-community relations)—both reports submitted at MIAMI
HEARINGS, November 12–13, 1991.

54   *See, e.g.,* Testimony of Dr. Larry Capp, psychologist, MIAMI HEAR-
INGS, November 12, 1991, at 214 (testifying that African American officers
have an advantage in patrolling African American communities, garner-
ing more trust and confidence and less suspicion and apprehension than
nonminority officers).

55   *See id.* at 213 (testifying that research has indicated that there
are fewer reports of brutality and citizen complaints when more black
officers patrol black communities); Testimony of Kathleen Worthy, UP-
PAC, MIAMI HEARINGS, November 13, 1991, at 485.

56   Testimony of Chief Calvin Ross, Miami Police Department,
MIAMI HEARINGS, November 13, 1991, at 455–56 ("[W]hat we are trying to
do is get a good mix. . . . I think it is very important that those . . . [who]
live . . . within our Hispanic communities . . . not only be exposed to
Hispanic officers, but . . . to our black officers and Anglo officers as well.
It is very healthy for the community as well as the officers. The same thing
holds true for the black community. I would certainly not like to see a
situation where as [*sic*] the only time our black community sees an Hispanic or Anglo officer is when there is a disturbance and we have to bring
all the manpower that we could muster. I think it is important that our
Hispanic and Anglo officers learn during peace time, how to deal with
these communities and be better [able] to deal with the community on a
day to day operation. . . .").

57   *See* Marc Cooper, *Dum Da Dum-Dum: L.A. Beware: The Mother
of All Police Departments Is Here to Serve and Protect,* VILLAGE VOICE, April
16, 1991, at 26 ("Los Angeles, among 252 American cities analyzed by a
recent University of Chicago study, was classified as 'hyper-segre-
gated.' ").

58   *See* ANDREW HACKER, TWO NATIONS, at 130 (1992).

59   *Id.*

60   In a 1992 survey of the employment of blacks, Hispanics, and
women in police departments of the 50 largest U.S. cities, the authors
note that they did not try to determine the reasons for the progress or lack
of progress in individual police departments, but they refer to previous
research finding that "the presence of an affirmative action plan, whether
voluntary or court-ordered, is a significant factor in increased employment of women and racial minorities." SAMUEL WALKER & K. B. TURNER, A
DECADE OF MODEST PROGRESS, at 2 (1992).

61   *See, e.g.,* Testimony of Msgr. Brian Walsh, Catholic Commission
for Social Advocates, MIAMI HEARINGS, November 12, 1991, at 191 (testify-

ing that minority representation in the police force should be supported, but is not a simple solution to problems in police-community relations, since, even in countries with no minority group based on ethnicity or race, poor relations exist between the police and poor people). Walsh recommends creation of a new law-enforcement culture to better relations between the police and (particularly) minority communities. *Id.*

62   *See, e.g.,* Testimony of Kathleen Worthy, UP-PAC, MIAMI HEARINGS, November 13, 1991, at 481–82 ("Why is it that these incidents which lead to killing, brutalizing, accusing of blacks by officers never happen when the arresting or investigating officers are black?").

63   *See, e.g.,* Testimony of Joe Persell, MIAMI HEARINGS, November 12, 1991, at 216–18, 223–24 (Persell, an African American, described an incident in which a black officer, in the course of a traffic stop, was insensitive—"offered to take [him] . . . to jail" and "seemed like he wanted to strike [him]. . . .").

64   *See* SIDNEY L. HARRING, POLICING A CLASS SOCIETY, at 13–21, 101–48 (1983) (discussing the role of the police in controlling the working class and the role of the police as strikebreakers).

65   *See, e.g.,* Testimony of Maj. Dennis R. Long, St. Louis County Police Department, ST. LOUIS HEARINGS, December 6, 1991, at 11–33.

66   *See* Testimony of John Pace, MIAMI HEARINGS, November 13, 1991, at 706, 713 (as president of an organization representing 450 corrections officers, recommends more minorities in decision-making positions).

67   *See, e.g.,* Testimony of Dr. Larry Capp, psychologist, MIAMI HEARINGS, November 12, 1991, at 252–53 (testifying research shows that "the biggest predictor of success in the police force is the intelligence score and that usually is correlated with higher . . . educational achievement. Although there are times when we have had people who score very high in terms of overall intelligence but who are only high school graduates. . . . The second highest factor that predicts success [is] . . . extroversion, being outgoing, being gregarious, being someone who likes people. . . ."); Testimony of Chief Michael McCrary, Signal Hill Police Department, LOS ANGELES HEARINGS, December 4, 1991, at 128 (testifying that he set new promotional standards which emphasize "a great deal of college"); Testimony of Helen Gros, executive director, Texas ACLU, HOUSTON HEARINGS, November 19, 1991, at 159 ("Officers must be selected for their maturity and their competence. Attempts to reduce standards for individuals entering law enforcement academies, must be thwarted."); Testimony of Mayor Kathryn Whitmire, HOUSTON HEARINGS, November 19, 1991, at 15 ("[W]e have increased educational requirements for our recruits. . . .").

68   *But see* Testimony of Chief Michael McCrary, Signal Hill Police Department, LOS ANGELES HEARINGS, December 4, 1991, at 141 (testifying that he is not sure his desire to have college-educated recruits is attainable, since a number of agencies that tried to impose this requirement

had problems in recruiting, the pay for police officers being less than what college graduates expect).

69 *See, e.g.,* Testimony of David Honig, general counsel, Miami-Dade Branch, NAACP, MIAMI HEARINGS, November 12, 1991, at 170 (testifying that two-thirds of black children in the Miami area attend predominantly black schools, despite a desegregation decree in 1972); Testimony of Gilbert Raiford, professor of social work, Barry University, MIAMI HEARINGS, November 13, 1991, at 619 (testifying that Miami has the highest dropout rate in the nation).

70 *See* Testimony of Chief Michael McCrary, Signal Hill Police Department, LOS ANGELES HEARINGS, December 4, 1991, at 141 ("[W]e make education a value. The City has a program where we reimburse for a college education . . . and for the number of units attained so they can make extra money. We give preference to shift assignments and work assignments for people that are going to school, to college.").

71 *See, e.g.,* Testimony of Dr. Larry Capp, psychologist, MIAMI HEARINGS, November 12, 1991, at 256–57 (testifying that, in response to a "hue and cry" after a crime wave in Miami in the early 1980s, hundreds of officers were hired without psychological testing (because testing was expected to slow down the hiring process); that as a result the force almost doubled in size, but many officers were hired without testing or after having been rejected by other departments; and that some of these remained on the force a decade later); Testimony of Kathleen Worthy, UP-PAC, MIAMI HEARINGS, November 13, 1991, at 485; Testimony of David Honig, general counsel, Miami-Dade Branch, NAACP, MIAMI HEARINGS, November 12, 1991, at 178 ("[W]e have to make sure that individuals with those . . . [psychologically disturbed] profiles are screened out very assiduously."); Testimony of Helen Gros, executive director, Texas ACLU, HOUSTON HEARINGS, November 19, 1991, at 159–60 ("Individuals who are not suited to deal with the variety of individuals in situations that a large city has to offer are simply not suited for law enforcement."); Testimony of Diane E. Watson, California state senator, LOS ANGELES HEARINGS, December 3, 1991, at 20 (testifying that the LAPD needs improved "cultural-sensitive psychological screening of and counseling of" officers).

72 *See, e.g.,* Testimony of Helen Gros, executive director, Texas ACLU, HOUSTON HEARINGS, November 19, 1991, at 159–60 ("Individuals who view their ultimate roles as enforcer, rather than peace officer, are ill-suited to law enforcement.").

73 *See, e.g.,* Testimony of Felicia Rodriguez, MIAMI HEARINGS, November 12, 1991, at 279 (recommending thorough investigation of backgrounds of officers before they work in the community); Testimony of Kathleen Worthy, UP-PAC, MIAMI HEARINGS, November 13, 1991, at 485 ("There is now a greater responsibility on elected officials to put in place a process for carefully screening police job applicants. . . ."); Testimony of Chief Michael McCrary, Signal Hill Police Department, LOS ANGELES

HEARINGS, December 4, 1991, at 141 (". . . I'm comfortable with the age of 21, if we carefully select our people. We do reject a number of people that are 21 to maybe 30, because [we] still think they're too immature.").

74   See Ralph Blumenthal, *Gay Officers Find Acceptance on New York's Police Force*, N.Y. TIMES, Feb. 21, 1993, at 1, 30.

75   See JURYWORK (Elissa Kraus & Beth Bonora, eds., 2d ed. 1986).

76   See Finding F5, *supra* 84–90.

77   See Testimony of Assistant Chief Hiram Contreras, Houston Police Department, HOUSTON HEARINGS, November 19, 1991, at 66–67.

78   *Id.*

79   See Testimony of Maj. Dennis R. Long, St. Louis County Police Department, ST. LOUIS HEARINGS, December 6, 1991, at 11.

80   See Testimony of Chief Ian Shipley, Chesapeake Police Department, NORFOLK HEARINGS, November 6, 1991, at 73; Testimony of Chief Charles Wall, Virginia Beach Police Department, NORFOLK HEARINGS, November 6, 1991, at 75; Testimony of Maj. Sheldon Darden, chief of operations, Norfolk Police Department, NORFOLK HEARINGS, November 6, 1991, at 77.

81   See, e.g., Testimony of David Shaheed, president-elect, Marion County Bar Association, INDIANAPOLIS HEARINGS, December 17, 1991, at 135 (advocating continued training, including sensitivity training of police officers despite their longevity on the force); Testimony of Helen Gros, executive director, Texas ACLU, HOUSTON HEARINGS, November 19, 1991, at 159 ("Officers must be trained not only in the essentials of law enforcement and Criminal Justice, but also in interpersonal relations."); Testimony of Deloyd Parker, executive director, SHAPE, HOUSTON HEARINGS, November 19, 1991, at 266 (testifying that officers presently on the force and on the streets should go back for further training in cultural differences); Testimony of Liz Morris, education coordinator, Houston Area Women's Center, HOUSTON HEARINGS, November 20, 1991, at 80 (testifying that the report of their family violence unit recommended mandatory training for all levels in the police department to eliminate sexist, racist, and homophobic behaviors, as well as increasing the number of female officers); Testimony of Mayor Xavier Suarez, MIAMI HEARINGS, November 12, 1991, at 50, 74.

82   See Testimony of Dr. Larry Capp, psychologist, MIAMI HEARINGS, November 12, 1991, at 213 (". . . [T]here is only so much that you can teach through [a] one week program about the black experience or the Haitian experience to non-minority officers and . . . so many factors in terms [of] nonverbal communications and nonverbal cues that simply can't be taught but simply have to be experienced.").

83   See id. at 233–34 ("We understand and we know from our experiences that people do change and that there is a tempering process that takes place. And in some cases there is a hardening process that takes place as well. . . . [P]olice officers . . . who patrol in high crime areas . . . deal with a high level of anxiety and stress on an ongoing basis. . . . They

tend not to have a whole lot of encounters with honest law abiding citizens. . . . In certain neighborhoods it is certainly not unusual for their attitudes to be reflected with suspiciousness towards everyone.").

84   *See* Testimony of Fred Taylor, director, Metro-Dade Police Department, MIAMI HEARINGS, November 12, 1991, at 123, and written report submitted at hearings, METRO-DADE VIOLENCE REDUCTION STUDY. In 1985 Metro-Dade and the Police Foundation in Washington, D.C., conducted a joint study to find "ways of reducing incidents of civilian use of force directed at officers, with the result of fewer incidents of officers using higher levels of force to protect themselves and control citizens." Taylor testified they looked at the kinds of contexts that generated a lot of complaints or use-of-force reports, identified five recurring types of situations, and began training on how to deal with them. The training includes communication skills, defensive tactics, firearm recertification, and interactive scenarios. According to Taylor, the department reviews and adds new scenarios. All sworn officers and sergeants undergo the training. According to the study, generally increasing citizen dissatisfaction peaked during the year training ended (1989), significantly declined the next year, and continues to decline. *Id.* For an explication of clinical education in a law school setting, *see, e.g.,* Abbe Smith, *Rosie O'Neill Goes to Law School: The Clinical Education of the Sensitive, New Age Public Defender,* 28 HARV-C.R.-C.L. L. REV. 1 (1993); Phyllis Goldfarb, *The Theory-Practice Spiral: The Ethics of Feminism and Clinical Education,* 75 MINN. L. REV. 1599 (1991); Anthony Amsterdam, *Clinical Legal Education—A 21st Century Perspective,* 34 J. LEGAL EDUC. 612 (1984); David Barnhizer, *The Clinical Method of Legal Instruction: Its Theory and Implementation,* 30 J. LEGAL EDUC. 67 (1979); Gary Bellow, *On Teaching the Teachers: Some Preliminary Reflections on Clinical Education as Methodology,* in CLINICAL EDUCATION FOR THE LAW STUDENT 374, 374–413 (1973).

85   *See* "WHERE THE INJURED FLY FOR JUSTICE," *supra* note 53 (recommending legislative amendment of statutes regarding training of officers, including taking steps to increase the amount of training in the characteristics of ethnic and cultural groups, to integrate the concept of racial and ethnic bias into other course curricula, to require instruction on communication and cross-cultural awareness for field-training officers, and to initiate "community interaction sessions").

86   *See, e.g.,* Testimony of Clarence Fisher, superintendent, Missouri State Highway Patrol, ST. LOUIS HEARINGS, December 6, 1991, at 23; Testimony of Maj. Dennis R. Long, St. Louis County Police Department, ST. LOUIS HEARINGS, December 6, 1991, at 23.

87   *See* Finding F3, *supra* 78–82. Some departments are attempting to move away from an "us versus them" attitude to a philosophy of cooperation with the community. *See also* SUSAN MICHAELSON ET AL., TOWARD A WORKING DEFINITION OF COMMUNITY POLICING (Program in Criminal Justice Policy and Management, Kennedy School of Government, Working Paper

88-05-09, 1988; George L. Kelling, *Police and Communities: The Quiet Revolution*, PERSPECTIVES ON POLICING, no. 1 (National Institute of Justice and Harvard University, 1988); Lee P. Brown, *Community Policing: A Practical Guide for Police Officials*, PERSPECTIVES ON POLICING, no. 12 (National Institute of Justice and Harvard University, 1989).

88   *See* Testimony of Rev. Joseph Green, vice-mayor, City of Norfolk, NORFOLK HEARINGS, November 6, 1991, at 19.

89   *See* Testimony of Col. David A. Robbins, president, St. Louis Board of Police Commissioners, ST. LOUIS HEARINGS, December 6, 1991, at 38–39 (testifying that COPS tries to "bridge the gap between resident and police" and is "leading our department to a stronger focus on customer satisfaction").

90   *See* Finding F3, *supra* 78–82.

91   *See, e.g.,* Testimony of Gilbert Raiford, professor of social work, Barry University, MIAMI HEARINGS, November 13, 1991, at 609 ("What we have here is fragmentation. Everybody gets a little bit of a lot of different things. They spread them out and it looks good. We have no big, comprehensive plans, we have nothing like that to pull this thing together. That is why there are no results. There is a lot of spinning of wheels, a lot of action, but nothing resulting from it that is positive and sustaining.").

92   *See* MALCOLM K. SPARROW ET AL., BEYOND 911, at 6 (1990).

93   *See id.*

94   *See id.*

95   *Id.* at 5.

96   *Id.*

97   *See* Testimony of Chief Calvin Ross, Miami Police Department, MIAMI HEARINGS, November 13, 1991, at 455 ("The police department operated in a vacuum going in to deal with what they consider as disorders or crime problems but the difference today . . . [is] we are listening from [*sic*] the citizens, their support and their ideas, how to best deal with the problems from their experiences in the community. They live there. They know the problems and they can best give us the input as to how to deal with it.").

98   *See* Testimony of Chief Jimmy R. Burke, Opa-Locka Police Department, MIAMI HEARINGS, November 12, 1991, at 97 ("[O]fficers have to park their vehicles and walk, get close to the citizens and remove the fear of contact on both sides."). *See also* SPARROW ET AL., *supra* note 11; SKOLNICK & BAYLEY, *supra* note 1.

99   HERMAN GOLDSTEIN, PROBLEM-ORIENTED POLICING (1990); SPARROW ET AL., *supra* note 11, at 17.

100   *See* GOLDSTEIN, *supra* note 99, at 32–34, 40–45.

101   *Id.* at 18–21, 45–47.

102   SPARROW ET AL., *supra* note 11, at 16.

103   *See id. See also* WILLIAM G. SPELMAN & DALE K. BROWN, CALLING THE

POLICE: CITIZEN REPORTING OF SERIOUS CRIME (National Institute of Justice, 1984).

104   See SPARROW ET AL., *supra* note 11, at 16.

105   See ERIC J. SCOTT, CALLS FOR SERVICE: CITIZEN DEMAND AND INITIAL POLICE RESPONSE (National Institute of Justice, 1981); WILLIAM SPELMAN ET AL., ON THE COMPETITIVE ENTERPRISE OF FERRETING OUT CRIME: THE NATURE OF THE PROBLEM, THE CAPACITY OF THE POLICE, AND THE ASSESSMENTS OF VICTIMS (Program in Criminal Justice Policy and Management, Kennedy School of Government, Working Paper 87-05-01, 1987).

106   See SKOLNICK & BAYLEY, *supra* note 1; SPARROW ET AL., *supra* note 11; GOLDSTEIN, *supra* note 99.

107   See SKOLNICK & BAYLEY, *supra* note 1.

108   See ST. CLAIR COMMISSION REPORT, at 129 (60% of our 50 largest cities have some form of civilian review; 10 of these programs have been adopted since 1988, 15 since 1986); Samuel Walker, "Civilian Review of the Police: A National Survey of the 50 Largest Cities" (#91-3, Focus: Criminal Justice Policy, University of Nebraska, 1991); Lee Brown, *The Civilian Review Board: Setting a Goal for Future Obsolescence*, INTERNATIONAL ASSOCIATION FOR CIVILIAN OVERSIGHT OF LAW ENFORCEMENT (IACOLE), Newsletter no. 16, September 1991.

109   ST. CLAIR COMMISSION REPORT, at 132.

110   CHRISTOPHER COMMISSION REPORT, at 171.

111   For example, Houston has the Citizens' Review Committee (CRC); Miami has the Office of Professional Compliance (OPC); Metro-Dade has the Independent Review Panel (IRP); Indianapolis has a Citizens' Complaint Office (CCO); and Virginia Beach had recently instituted the first civilian board in Virginia history at the time of the hearings.

112   Testimony of Michael Zinzun, Coalition against Police Abuse, Committee for Justice, LOS ANGELES HEARINGS, December 3, 1991, at 100. *See also* Testimony of Mary Redd, Urban League, NORFOLK HEARINGS, November 6, 1991, at 177 (testifying that a citizen review panel would allow the police to "learn from the experiences of . . . citizens").

113   Testimony of Brian Reeder, executive director, Indianapolis Citizens' Complaint Office, INDIANAPOLIS HEARINGS, December 17, 1991, at 73. *See also* Testimony of Deloyd Parker, executive director, SHAPE, HOUSTON HEARINGS, November 19, 1991, at 233, 254 (urging the creation of a real civilian review board with "teeth").

114   *But see* Testimony of Brian Reeder, executive director, Indianapolis Citizens' Complaint Office, INDIANAPOLIS HEARINGS, December 17, 1991, at 93–94 (testifying that CCO does not receive funding for its own investigative staff, so IAD investigates all complaints).

115   Among the cities in which hearings were held, only the Indianapolis Citizens' Complaint Office has subpoena power. *But see* Testimony of West Pomeray, MIAMI HEARINGS, November 12, 1991, at 57 (recommending subpoena power); Testimony of Diane E. Watson, Cali-

fornia state senator, LOS ANGELES HEARINGS, December 3, 1991, at 23 (recommending subpoena power).

116   *See, e.g.,* Testimony of Assistant Chief Phyllis Wunsche, Houston Police Department, IAD, HOUSTON HEARINGS, November 19, 1991, at 112 (testifying that in Houston officers can be ordered to answer questions in administrative proceedings, but not in criminal investigations). Wunsche said that officers "do cooperate" and that police departments supply the review board with the information it needs. *Id.* Where an officer may face criminal charges as well as review board investigation, care must be taken not to secure the officer's testimony by a promise of immunity, which could hamper a criminal prosecution (the problem Oliver North's prosecutors encountered in pursuing criminal charges after North testified before Congress in the Iran-Contra hearings).

117   *See* Testimony of Judy Steen Davis, MIAMI HEARINGS, November 13, 1991, at 567.

118   *See, e.g.,* Testimony of Helen Gros, executive director, Texas ACLU, HOUSTON HEARINGS, November 19, 1991, at 179–80; Testimony of Mayor Kathryn Whitmire, HOUSTON HEARINGS, November 19, 1991, at 48–49; Testimony of Joe Persell, MIAMI HEARINGS, November 12, 1991, at 225–26; Testimony of Rosa Rondon, MIAMI HEARINGS, November 12, 1991, at 269.

119   *See, e.g.,* Testimony of West Pomeray, MIAMI HEARINGS, November 12, 1991, at 59.

120   *See, e.g.,* Testimony of Rev. James Taylor, INDIANAPOLIS HEARINGS, December 18, 1991, at 151.

▲ INDEX ▲

police shootings in, 12, 43, 58
Professional Compliance Bureau, 46
racism in, 22, 23
ranks obtained by minorities, 91, 92, 94
recruitment policies in, 87, 90
verbal abuse and harassment in, 40
Missouri State Highway Patrol. *See also* St. Louis
citizen complaints in, 51
community policing in, 79, 81
cultural diversity training in, 95
recruitment policies in, 85, 88
Moore, Mark H., 113, 114

NAACP, 1, 3–4, 7
National Black Police Association (NBPA), 69, 75, 76, 77
National Center on Institutions and Alternatives, 24–25
National Conference of Christians and Jews, 98
National Institute on Drug Abuse, 25
National Organization of Black Law Enforcement Executives (NOBLE), 76, 77, 78, 98
Neighborhood-oriented policing. *See* Community-oriented policing
New York City, 12, 92
Norfolk
citizen complaints in, 60
community-oriented policing in, 125
community relations in, 101
excessive and deadly force in, 27
minorities in police departments, 83
NAACP hearings in, 3
police misconduct in, 29, 44, 48
racism in, 19–20
ranks obtained by minorities, 94
recruitment policies in, 86, 87, 88, 122

People United to Lead the Struggle for Equality (PULSE), 30–31

Perjury by police, 55, 77
Philadelphia, police dogs in, 34
Police conduct and community relations. *See* Community relations and police conduct
Police culture, 15–17
Police dogs, 28, 32–34
Police misconduct, 3. *See also* Citizen complaints; Excessive or deadly force; False charges and retaliatory actions; Stop and frisk; Verbal abuse and harassment
in Boston, 45
in Chesapeake, 48–49
civil lawsuits as remedy, 65–68
FBI investigation of, 64
in Houston, 46
incidence of abuse and race, 68–70
Judiciary Committee report on, 4–6
in Long Beach, 47–48
in Los Angeles, 4, 39, 44–45
in Miami and Dade County, 31, 40, 46–47, 49
monitoring procedures, 43–50, 84
NBPA and NOBLE action against, 76, 77, 78
in Norfolk, 29, 44, 48
in personnel evaluation, 114–115
public opinion concerning, 5, 6, 74–78
racially motivated, 7–15, 19–24, 82–84
rules defining and prohibiting, 112
in St. Louis, 48
in Virginia Beach, 49
Police officers, impaired, 32
Police officers, killing of, 25, 106
Police professionalism, 113–114, 115
Police shootings, 12, 28. *See also* Excessive or deadly force
in Houston, 32
incidence of and race, 69
in Indianapolis, 29